BRAHMA'S

PUSHKAR

ANCIENT INDIAN PILGRIMAGE

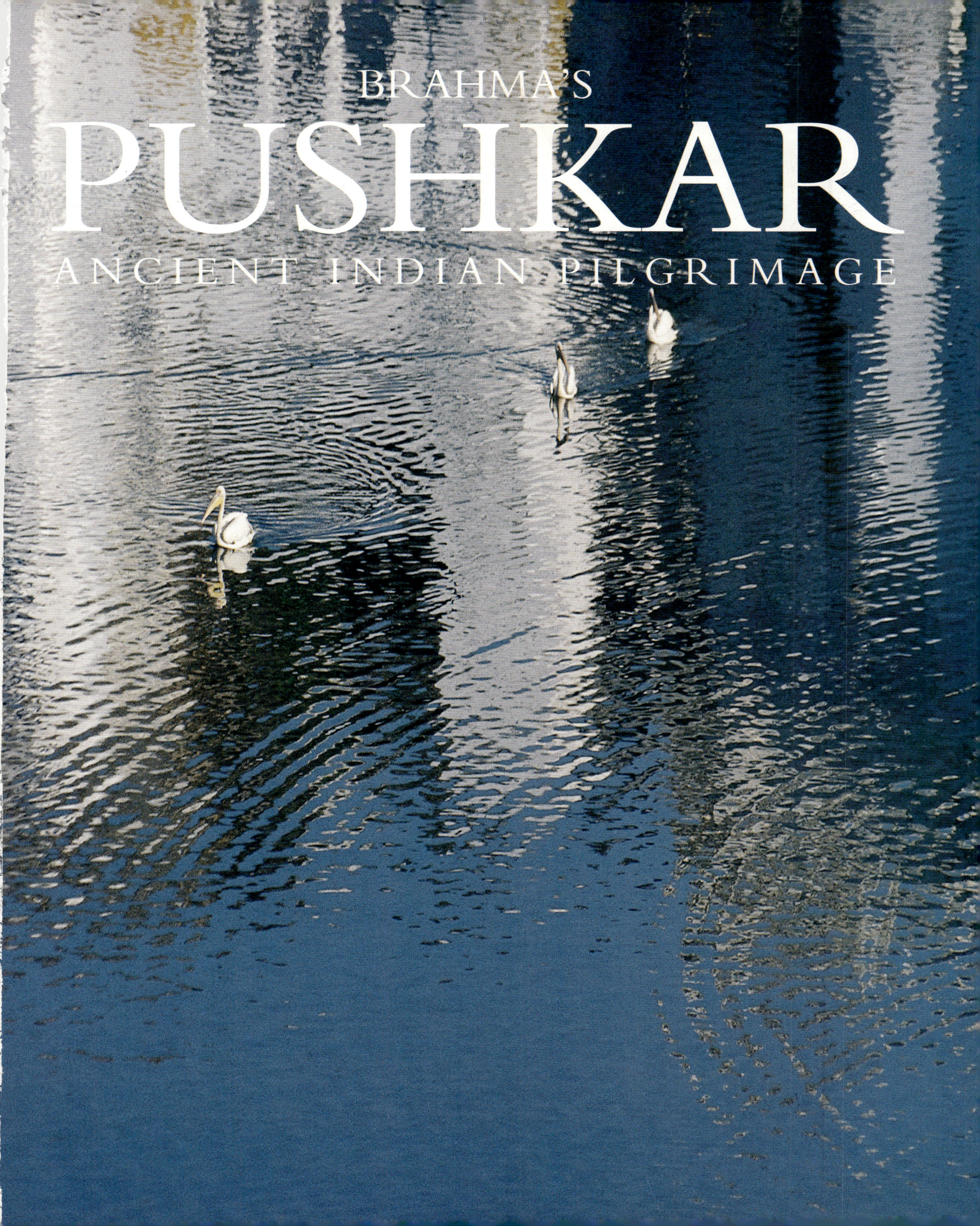

BRAHMA'S

ANCIENT INDIAN PILGRIMAGE

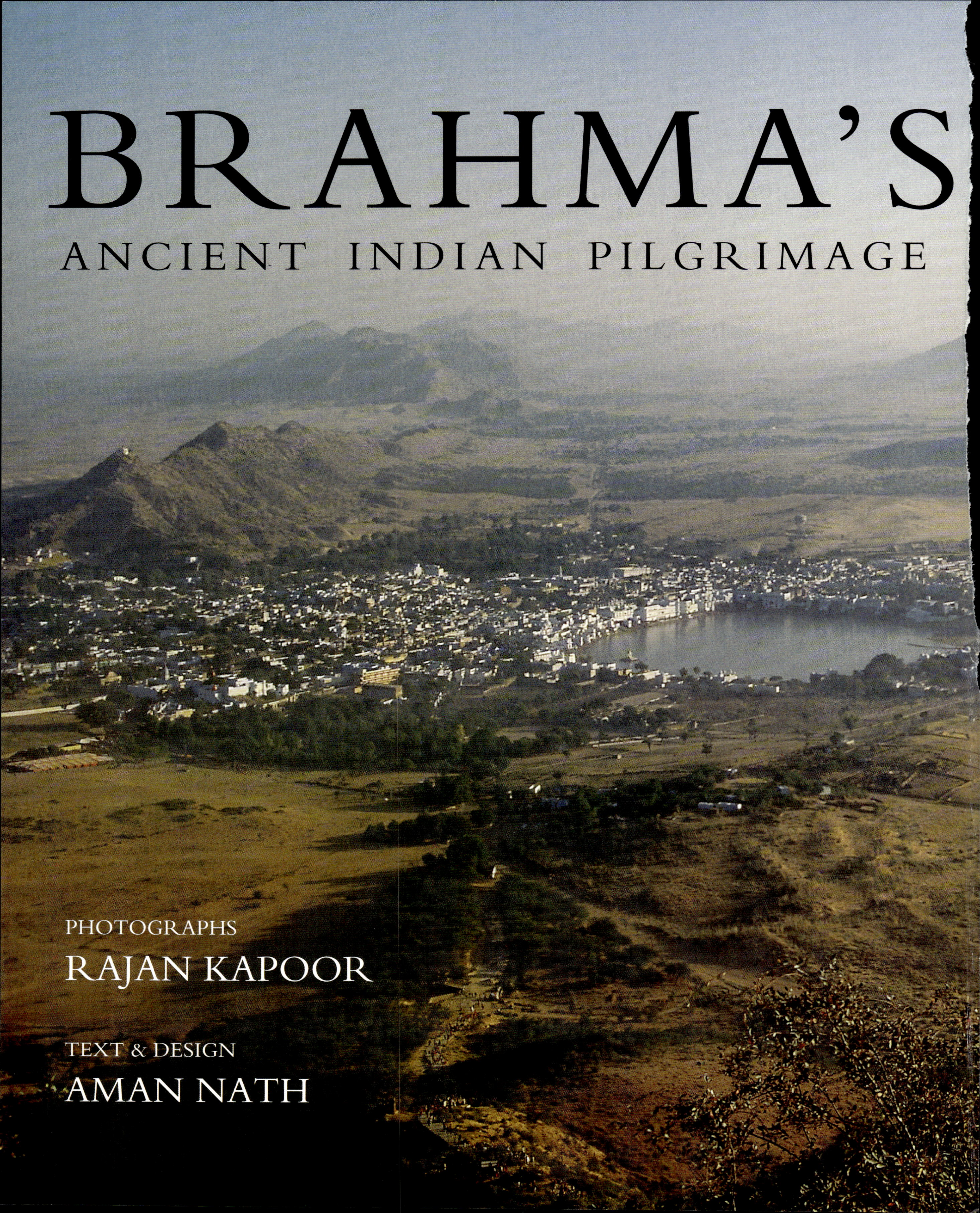

PHOTOGRAPHS
RAJAN KAPOOR

TEXT & DESIGN
AMAN NATH

PUSHKAR

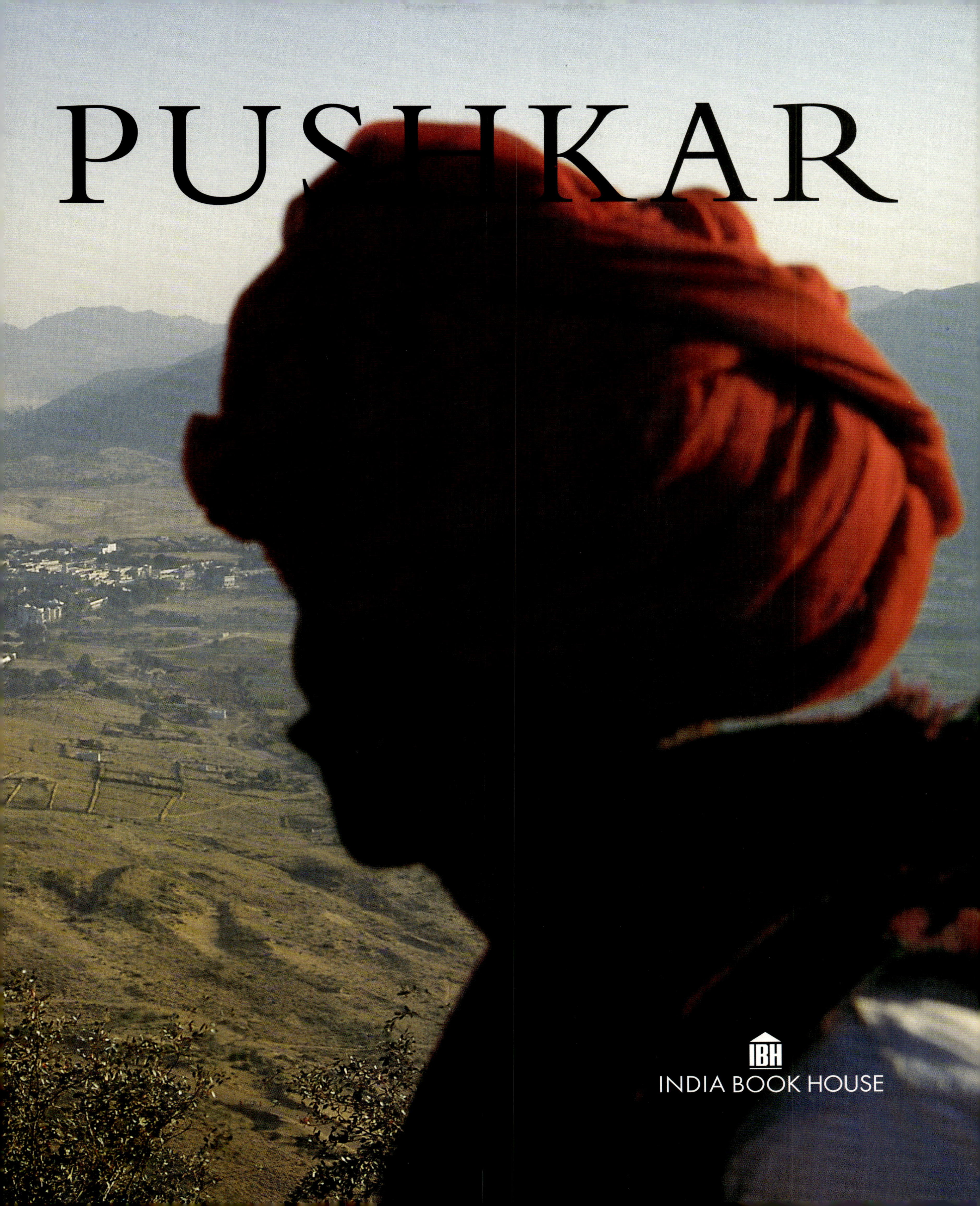

INDIA BOOK HOUSE

To my father from whom I inherited the love of art and to my mother who taught me that creation is one of the best recreations. — RAJAN KAPOOR

For Aadya, little goddess of future joys and hopes. — AMAN NATH

ISBN 81-7508-371-9

DESIGN Aman Nath
EDITOR Shernaz Vasunia

PROCESSING Reproscan
PRINTING JAK Printers

PUBLISHED BY
India Book House Publishing
22, Mahalaxmi Chambers
Bhulabhai Desai Road
Mumbai 400 026, India
Tel 91 22 2352 3827 Fax 91 22 2353 8406
E-mail publishing@ibhworld.com

NOTE *Names of temples, caves and stepwells around the circumambulatory routes at Pushkar have been spelt phonetically, in order to facilitate easy recognition of sites both for the traveller and the pilgrim.*

CONTENTS

PROLOGUE *"...even the 'Gods' hinged on the creativity of man"*

ABOVE *Veiled Rajasthani women add colour to the eternal landscape of Pushkar.*

BELOW *Pushkar lies at the heart of India's westernmost state of Rajasthan, 15 kilometres west of Ajmer.*

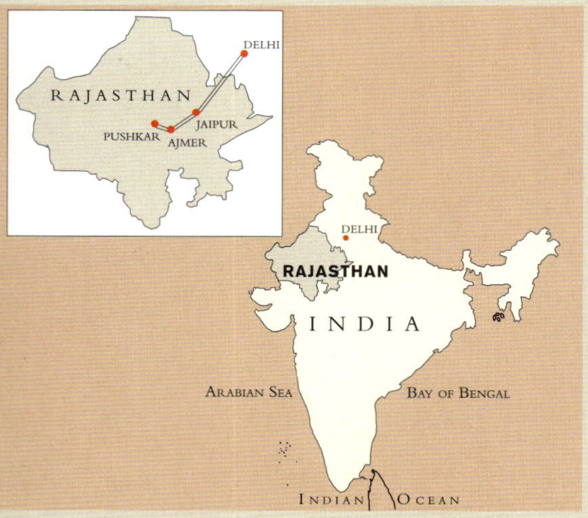

Hinduism is a-historical in its origins. Practised as a way of life over millennia, its followers have enriched their beliefs and rituals by being inclusive and assimilative of other ways of worship. No single book, oral doctrine, or individual revelation defines its nebulous parameters. A look at the recorded history of the 'civilized' world, shows that mankind has not enjoyed much flexibility in choosing its gods – except perhaps those born within the Hindu faith. However, while the Hindus continued to evolve the worship of a staggering range of personal deities, their dharma – as opposed to a rigid religion – has long known the wisdom of 'one god'. At the human level, caste restrictions may have constricted social mobility, but the macro vision of the cosmic creator remained.

In the prehistoric Indian subcontinent, which cradled and nurtured one of the world's first civilizations in the Indus Valley – and later on saw the fusion of many cultures – the Hindus learnt the importance of keeping alive the democracy of choosing one's gods from all those which were created on earth and 'brought' to their land. They knew that all paths eventually lead to the omnipresent one. The significance of this early realization cannot be stressed enough, especially to those not raised within this context: to see only a part as the whole.

Within this universal reverence, Hinduism has also, arguably, the most copious body of literature which questions or denies the presence of god, and gives vent to open blasphemy. The *nastikas*, or the atheists, ran parallel with the priestly class. They rejected 'inference' because it was based on pre-suppositions, as also 'testimony', because it involved inference or thinking in a circle. The *nastikas* followed hedonism, skepticism, cynicism – and yet they, along with the agnostics, were accepted by Hinduism as part of its process of liberating thought. Throughout, India has produced schismatics and protestants, dissenters and rebels, who shook Hinduism's orthodoxy but were not excommunicated from it, amply demonstrating its open elasticity and level of tolerance.

However, Hinduism went through a period of uncertainty in the early centuries of the Christian era. The theory of *advaita* (non-duality), officially re-propounded by Adi Shankaracharya in the 8th-9th centuries CE, emerged as a challenge to Buddhism, ritualism and other dualistic Hindu sects such as Mimansa. Shankaracharya travelled widely all over India, and set up four *mathas*, or monasteries, in Shringeri near Mysore in the south, Dwarka in the west, Puri in the east, and Badrinath in the north. But, as is natural in an evolved and evolving religion, his *advaita* was contested by theistic Vaishnava, Shaiva and Shakta sects as well as ritualistic cults, and his contribution to the religious life of the Hindu is still a matter of debate among theologians.

The religious life of a Hindu is not confined to the worship of a personal god. Dharma governs the emotional, economic, political and spiritual pursuits of all Hindus. The unique feature of the Hindu moral and ethical code is that it incorporates the negative as well as positive commandments, i.e. the four *purusharthas:* dharma (righteousness), *artha* (creating wealth), *kama* (procreation for continuity) and moksha (liberation). Furthermore, the all-embracing religious life of the Hindu does not confine the concept of the sacred or divine to the unworldly. For the Hindu, the earth as a whole is sacred – with particular places being particularly sacred. There are sacred hills, sacred groves, sacred trees, sacred animals, sacred rivers and sacred lakes. Places like Pushkar became sacred because of their mythological associations, or simply because their natural setting inspired noble thoughts:

In the valleys of hills and on the confluences of rivers,
the wisdom of the Brahman [the 'absolute'] was born.

– RIGVEDA, vii.6.28

The trinity of the Hindus, and the 3,339 *devatas* (gods) of the Rigveda (or 330 million of the Puranas) bless over 800 million Hindus on this earth – not all of them practitioners, a ratio of less than three devotees per god. This certainly makes for an amazing democracy of choices! As Shashi S Sharma writes in his well-reasoned treatise *Oh My God:* "It is possible to have as many visions of God as there are men...every man can have his very own *ishta devata,* a god that he fervently wishes to have as his own. The meaning of the word *ishta* corresponds to 'that which it wishes for' or 'the occurrence of that which is desired'. In this *ishta devata* lies that aspect of God which reveals itself to man in a specific act of appreciation...a 'second-hand' religiosity [the 'revelation' of another] was never considered a noble vocation in India. Man stood resplendent at the centre of creation, and all manifested phenomena and even the 'Gods' hinged on the creativity of man."

Pushkar, as the *tirthaguru,* or guru of all pilgrimage sites, represents this multiplicity of Hindu choices; an evolved and democratic form of monotheism. An average Hindu has no problems with the apparently contradictory doctrines of monism, monotheism and polytheism.

This abundance of gods at Pushkar may be easier to understand if seen as the multiple paths to the eventual goal. As a priest at Pushkar explained, "Idols and rituals are like ladders and scaffolding. Once you get to the abstract heights, you don't need them." This modern-day statement is a reflection of Shankaracharya's view of the relevance of worship as a stage of spiritual progress towards the realization of the 'absolute'.

For many, travelling, reading and exposure may already have rid this profusion of Hindu gods off their pejorative connotations of an archaic and confused multiplicity. For others, this may be an occasion to finally try and fathom that the Hindus are practitioners of a religion which has been around for a few millennia more than most others – which fructifies into what may well remain for some novices an incomprehensible diversity.

Hinduism has been assimilative rather than exclusivist in nature and NK Bose rightly calls it a "Federation of religious beliefs and practices." It has also been said that Hinduism is like a banyan tree whose branches have taken root while the original form is untraceable (Sinha and Saraswati). Readers may find the plethora of Hindu legends and mythologies quite bewildering. As the Puranas were coined for the masses, many of these are exaggerated – even absurd beyond belief – but their allegorical significance is abundantly evident. Rejecting them instantly as superstitious stories can distance readers from the deeper truths of the Vedas and the Upanishads. As Greg Bailey reiterates, "The Hindu epics and Puranas contain a vast repository of mythology... utilizing a common stock of motifs and imagery.... However, the myths themselves are not subordinate to the motifs.... To grasp the meaning (or meanings) of these myths it is essential not only to have a thorough knowledge of the motifs, but also to penetrate beneath them to the value systems which are expressed through the myths and also shape them. The existence of such (implicit) value systems becomes clear after a reading of the myths and the didactic literary material which is scattered throughout the same texts in which the myths appear."

Pushkar represents this wealth – as Life – in all its celebratory bounty. If nothing else, it is an open-ended lesson in the acceptance of diverse and even contradictory traditions. As S Radhakrishnan, the erudite, second president of India, had written, "Tolerance is the homage which the finite mind pays to the inexhaustibility of the Infinite."

Etymologically, 'religion' means 'that which binds one back to the origin' (from the Latin *re,* back and *ligare,* to bind). Interestingly, the present at Pushkar can also take you to that past.

THE SUBTLE PHONETICS

BRAHM, *also* BRĀHMAṆDA The Cosmos

BRAHMĀ The Creator

BRAHMAN The Absolute

BRĀHMAṆ A Member of the Priestly Class

THE BRĀHMAṆAS Religious Scriptures

BELOW *In secular India, it is not just the Hindus who have come to have a deep understanding of that One God. Truckers of different religions spread the message,* 'Sab ka malik ek' – *everyone's lord is one – using the Urdu word* malik *for God.*

ETERNAL PUSHKAR

The antiquity of Pushkar is testified in the ancient epics

Everything was pure in the Krita age;
in Treta, Pushkar became sacred;
in Dwapara, Kurukshetra –
and in the Kali age, Ganga became sacred.

— MAHABHARATA (Vana Parva, 83-90)

BRAHMA, LORD OF ALL CREATION, BUT...

PRECEDING PAGES *Haloed with the morning mist, the sacred lake and pilgrimage site of Pushkar awakens in the morning.*

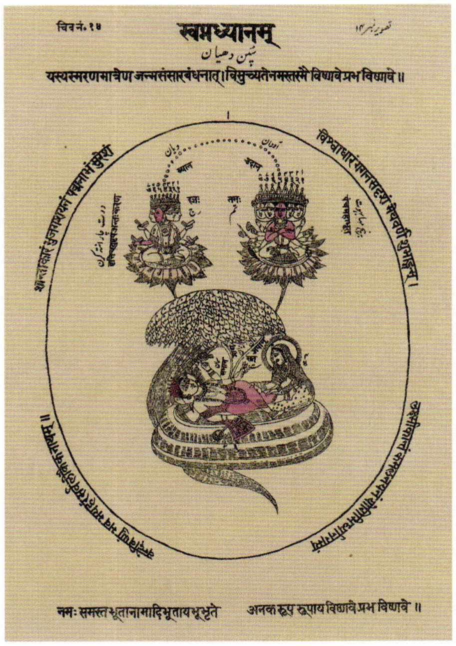

ABOVE *A 19th-century Indian lithograph conceptualizes the cosmic egg and the primordial waters with its own ingenuity.*

BELOW *A mid-19th-century French illustrator tries to visualize the appearance of Brahma from the cosmic egg using a mix of Jewish/Christian imagery of Satan and an angel with that of an Oriental pagan god.*

Recurring motifs appear in the mythology of the epics and the Puranas. These motifs are not subordinate to the myths, but continue to provide their content, thereby suggesting a dharma. This does not become a rigid belief of dos and don'ts. Perhaps, more importantly, these motifs and myths have got embedded in the psyche-conscience and over the centuries, become a silent, inborn code of righteousness for Hindus. In reading or studying these motif-based myths, it needs hardly to be argued that they achieved their moral purpose. But that they made the Hindu mind eternally open like a lake – to rain, rivulets, even floods – shows the contemplative depths of wisdom from which they were sourced.

INCEST & ITS LOGIC

When Brahma's golden egg of creation, the *hiranyagarbha*, emerged from the waters of the great flood, he was alone. To posit the act of creation to a single being, the supreme spirit, is to state the problem itself. The impossibility of the situation – reproduction through *purusha*, or a single male energy – becomes the logic for creation through incest. From the passion of his lust, Brahma was obliged to give birth to a daughter, Sarasvati, and then proceed to marry her. In another myth from the Matsya Purana, Brahma created Shatarupa from half of his body and then accepted her as his wife. She was so beautiful that he couldn't, even for a moment, keep his eyes off her. As he turned to admire her in every direction, he grew four heads. Finally, when she flew into the sky, hiding from the lustful glance of her father/husband, he looked up and a fifth head sprouted on top. These acts are immoral only if human standards are applied, explains the Matsya Purana (chapter III), for gods beget children in a different way.

THE EVOLUTION OF BRAHMA

The heights to which Hindu philosophical debate and introspection had evolved needs a certain degree of initiation before it can be comprehended and absorbed. In a very subtle and unconscious transformation, the first steps in the creation of the concept of Creator escaped even those who conceived it.

The evolution of Brahma from a mere concept to that of the Creator, and then as part of the composite trinity, is an oft-ignored aspect. However, this process is important in order to understand the association of Brahma vis-à-vis Pushkar.

Brahma is mentioned in the Shatapatha Brahmana of circa 8th century BCE. However, as the masculine personification of *brahm* (the impersonal, absolute spirit), he finds extensive mention in texts from the Rigveda onwards. From this abstract, cosmic spirit, *brahm*, comes Brahma, the male god. However, there is no consensus among scholars to assert that in Vedic literature the neuter word *brahm* actually predates the masculine Brahma. But, Greg Bailey states that "there are compelling reasons to view his [Brahma's] early development as a process of apotheosization of the Brahman priest." The priest's function in the *shrauta* (a Vedic sacrifice) was, as L Silburn sums up, "Like a chief of the orchestra he directs the entire ceremony."

The *brahm* of the later Vedic literature defied description as a cosmic concept – which was grammatically neuter. At best, he was an anthropomorphism for the sky or space – an aspect that Brahma's five heads (later four) came to symbolize, literally describing four directions and space.

Since the Vedas were largely related to an era where sacrifice was all-important, the *purusha*, or the primeval being, was offered as a sacrifice – almost as a self-sacrifice/immolation of the demiurge – to establish in himself an equation of *brahm* and *atma*. "Finally, the most definite expression for the object of man's search was found in the concept of *atma*.....the microcosmic obverse of the coin of which Brahm is the macrocosm-reverse", writes Sukumari Bhattacharji.

Brahma grows from Prajapati (another important Vedic deity) on the one hand, and from Brihaspati on the other, to gradually emerge as a masculine concept in the epic period.

ABOVE *After the period of the Ramayana and the Mahabharata, Brahma is usually shown as an old man, described as a grandfather, while Shiva (seen with Parvati) and Vishnu retain their youthfulness, as also depicted in this British etching published by G & WB Whitaker in 1824.*

Both in the Ramayana and the Mahabharata, Brahma clearly emerges as the male Creator-Grandfather, *pitamaha* of the *pitris* (ancestors), or father of the fathers. One can thus sense that in his very evolution he is already a 'spent force'. He seems part of a remote and archaic antiquity. Many instances of his detachment – in order to be liberated – are seen in the Mahabharata with the evident danger of his being made redundant. He becomes, according to Dumezil, consubstantial with the sacrifice – which he himself was – thereby obliterating himself.

According to the Milinda Panho of the Buddhist period, all men of those days – monks, itinerant teachers and Brahmans – were worshippers of Brahma. But soon after, in the Agama Sutta of the Digha Nikaya, we are told how Brahma falsely imagines that he is the highest god of all, the eternal Creator of the universe, when, according to Buddhist teaching, the universe evolves and declines according to natural law, writes AL Basham.

Finally, when neo-Brahmanism surged forward after the Buddhist intervention, Hinduism united India as never before. Brahma, who had by then been divulged of his active powers, "removed from the mortals by a whole generation of gods, and thus at two removes from men," also made a resurgence from his dark arena of neglect to squarely being at the centre of the neo-Brahmanical trinity (Bhattacharji). In this aloof, patriarchal role, Brahma sacrifices his status and unwittingly becomes the meeting point between Shiva and Vishnu in many legends, as also the reconciler of all contradictory principles and rival cults. Bhattacharji elaborates: "The Tantric worshippers regard Shakti as the *maya* of Brahma. The Shaivas worship Rudra-Shiva as the spiritual son of Brahma. Thus Brahma became the name for the final realization of all sects."

BELOW *A detail of a 19th-century painting from Jaipur of the* darbar *of Ganga, in which the trinity stand in attendance. The wise Brahma (middle) appears as a sage with four white beards.*

Brahma's mythology never really became a separate subject of Indian theology. With the exception of a few references in the Upanishads and the late Brahmanas, Brahma is virtually absent from Vedic literature. At best, "Brahma performs distinctive roles within the total ensemble of epic and Puranic mythology," observes Greg Bailey, whose singular work, *The Mythology of Brahma* is perhaps the most comprehensive work on this deity.

In many myths of creation, the improbable is often posited as a rigid postulation – irrevocably beyond the known logic of society. But being in the realm of faith – much like the Immaculate Conception – that it was in the first place, it is never meant to be questioned by reasoning.

To know how old the recorded myth of creation is, one can look at it philologically. The Vedic genealogy of Brahma can be traced back to Tvashtra who is called *janitra* (progenitor), and to Prajapati, called *prajayanitra* – also meaning progenitor, its cognate in Latin, the language of the ancient Roman empire. Its Vedic-Prakrit-Sanskrit beginnings talk of its antiquity. In both traditions – Vedic and Roman – it means ancestor or predecessor, a mantle Brahma took on easily.

BRAHMA & SHIVA, PUSHKAR & KASHI/BANARAS

It is an interesting study to juxtapose Brahma and Shiva, and their relative importance as part of the trinity, as well as independently.

ABOVE *An 1845 etching from a French publication,* Inde *by De Jancigny, Dubois & Raymond Xavier, shows Brahma with Sarasvati on one side and his swan on the other (top), while Shiva, Parvati and Ganesha are worshipped (bottom).*

The Kashi Rahasya, written by Shaivites to increase the importance of Kashi/Banaras, draws a parallel between Brahmanda – the cosmos – and Kashi. Just as all the gods and souls take refuge in the Brahmanda, so do all *tirthas* and the seven cities take refuge in Kashi. In Kashi it is said – and the Brahmans at Pushkar may not agree with this – that when Brahma weighed their city against all the gods in heaven, the heavens rose up in the balancing pan to touch the sky, while Kashi touched the ground!

Just as there is a Brahma Ghat at Pushkar, there is one at Kashi. About the latter, Diana L Eck notes, "Princep's illustration of Brahma Ghat from the early 1800s shows a very busy ghat for bathing and washing. Saris hang from the lofty turrets to dry, and wood is stacked high on the ghat, suggesting that perhaps cremations took place on this section of the riverfront too." Later it seems to have declined in importance.

Even though Brahma has no cult at Kashi, his myths are recalled at the relevant sites: The Brahmeshvara and the Dashashvamedheshvara *lingas* at the Dashashvamedha Ghat in Kashi are believed to have been established by Brahma after he persuaded King Divodasa to sponsor 10 *ashvamedha* sacrifices. The benefit of these sacrifices was reaped by the sponsor king and not Brahma or the Brahmans.

Another legend mentions that after honouring Shiva, Brahma is said to have settled in Kashi. The Hiranyagarbha and Sangameshvara *lingas*, also attributed to Brahma, stand at the confluence of the two rivers, Varuna and Ganga, and within the precincts of the Adi Keshava Temple.

PANCHMUKHI TO CHATURMUKHA BRAHMA

There are 12 *jyotirlingas* in all, but Kashi – where Shiva's fiery *linga* pierced the three worlds – became the epitome of effulgence, making it the city of light. Brahma and Vishnu wondered about the limits of this '*linga* of light'. Brahma flew up on his swan to search for its end, while Vishnu bored the earth as *varaha*, the wild boar incarnation, for its beginning. On returning, Brahma lied about having seen the top to maintain the Creator's conceit, and in anger, Shiva chopped off Brahma's fifth head. Vishnu honestly conceded to Shiva's superiority (see miniature painting on p.15).

BELOW *A mid-19th-century painting from Jaipur of Bhairava with his weapons and Brahma's skull stuck in one of his right hands.*

In the Kashi Khanda version of this myth, Shiva punishes this arrogance by chopping off Brahma's fifth head which had stuck out on top, by taking the fearsome form of Kala Bhairava. Since Brahma represents the archetypal Brahman – whose killing is considered as one of the five great sins – his skull sticks to Shiva/Bhairava's hand (see left). After wandering the whole land, Bhairava returns to Banaras. His retribution and atonement completed, the skull falls loose at Kapalamochana, north of the Matsyadari river, now a pilgrimage point in Kashi.

Once when all the worlds had drowned under a single ocean, nothing but darkness prevailed. Bhagavan, the supreme being, too slept for many thousands of his nights – each equalling a thousand human years. At the end of that night, Bhagavan (Brahma) took on the attribute of *rajas*, activity, while another being, Purusha, or the male creative energy as Shiva, took a form with the attribute of *tamas*, darkness. Then the supreme spirit, *mahatma*, created egotism or *ahankara*. Affected by their individual pride, Brahma and Shiva quarrelled over their superiority. Brahma asked Shiva embarrassing questions. Finally, Shiva was defeated and bowed his head but Brahma continued to chide him. "You have three eyes, and yet, your attribute is darkness." Shiva was angered and, opening his third eye, attempted to burn Brahma, who arrogantly retorted: "When you beat on water, bubbles will appear, but do the bubbles have any prowess?" The insulted Shiva plucked off one head of Brahma with the tip of his fingernails, leaving him with four heads (see below). This is the head that stuck to Shiva/Bhairava's palm till it was atoned-for in Kashi.

ABOVE *A 19th-century painting from Sirohi of Brahma saluting Shiva (in the foreground), after his fifth head is struck off. In this narrative miniature, he is shown fleeing in the background.*

BRAHMA & THE CURSE OF SHIVA

Sarasvati was the daughter of Brahma, and later became his wife. In this incredulous myth of creation, Brahma, as the Creator, had the daunting and unenviable task of creating all by himself. So he used his own heat and vital fluids to produce a beautiful daughter Sarasvati. (In an alternative legend, lusting after the *apsara,* or nymph, Urvashi, Brahma ejaculated into an earthen pot which bore him a daughter.) Lusting after his daughter is one reason why Shiva cursed Brahma not to be worshipped. "It is Brahma's braggadocio that earns him the curse of Shiva

ABOVE *A wood-carved window grille from the 19th century depicting the cosmic serpent Sheshanaga, on whose eternal coils Vishnu sleeps. In this version, the preserver gives birth to the Creator, from a lotus which sprouts from his navel.*

FACING PAGE *A mid-19th-century miniature painting from Bikaner of Shiva manifesting himself as* lingodbhavamurti *in the* jyotirlinga *legend.*

BELOW *This painting depicts Vishnu Narayana's edge over Brahma, who appears from a lotus in his navel. In this version, Shiva is shown seated above them both on a crescent moon.*

never to have a cult of his own," writes Eck. According to another legend, the five-headed Brahma presided over the wedding of Shiva and Parvati as Prajapati. So overcome was he by the bride's beauty that in the heat of the moment he soiled his loincloth. Shiva, aghast at this obvious lack of control, struck off one of Brahma's heads while cursing him with a lack of progeny. Yet, in other versions Brahma has many sons!

BRAHMA'S DECLINE

In the many mythological tales of the Puranas, the Brahmans, who composed them, finally put the gods to reason. They reckoned that, for one, the legends must first appeal to what we may today call their 'market audience', and secondly, to perpetuate their brand loyalty, Shiva or Vishnu (depending on the sectarian preference of the writer) must prove his superiority over the other.

Brahma, the pre-eminent god of the post-Vedic times, the Creator, could not suddenly be left out of this hierarchical race, so he was included in the pantheistic trinity. But, beyond that, there was nothing he could offer his worshippers. Or, more appropriately, looking at it from the 'buyer's viewpoint' – there was nothing they could hope to ask from him. The Creator, having created, could add nothing to his creation. The Shiva and Vishnu Puranas, besides inventing simple tales of rivalry which appealed to lay worshippers, also let the tension aggravate to inane tirades against each other. In this, Brahma too was not spared. After having completed his thankless job of creation he was superceded, often as are old parents – relegated to pass solitary time on their own. As if this were not enough, tales of Brahma's intended incest with his daughter, his lust for Shiva's wife and his blatant lying in the *jyotirlinga* legend – all placed him almost at the human level of a sinner. The Shaivites and Vaishnavites eventually won the race for their own 'brand names'.

In few other religions of the world is the Creator involved in legends where his shortcomings are exposed in a way akin to the humans whom he has created. Brahma, fashioned within the frailties and pitfalls which mark common humans, does not escape punishment for complacency, neglect, conceit, infidelity and lust. The various legends on Brahma losing his fifth head have already been examined. Thus, in most of the Puranas, Brahma is called *chaturmukha*, or four-faced. The chief idol in the Brahma Temple at Puskhar also represents him with four heads.

COSMIC & EARTHLY NAMES DERIVED FROM BRAHMA

Since Brahma was the lord of all creation, the cosmos was naturally given his name: Brahmanda, or Brahma's cosmic golden egg. In society too, the priestly class, considered first among the four castes, designated themselves as Brahman – the microcosm of the macrocosmic Brahma.

Then again, the Brahmanas, as theological manuals of the later Vedic period, represent the oldest prose in any Indo-European language. Written by and for the Brahmans, they are manuals laying down detailed procedures for the performance of different rituals. Each Veda has one or more Brahmanas attached to it.

On the terrestrial plain, it is interesting to see where Brahma's name is physically ascribed to a territorial region, a city, or a river. The term Brahmakshetra used in the Mahabharata and the Vayu Purana has been traced to Kurukshetra where the Pandavas and the Kauravas fought their epic battle – also called Brahmarshi Deesha or the Brahmavarta of Manu. Then there is Brahmapura (which the 7th-century Chinese traveller, Hiuen Tsang called the Po-lo-lih-mo-pu-lo), comprising parts of the Garhwal and Kumaon districts, in Uttaranchal. Brahmatirtha and Brahmasara are among the names that appear for Pushkar in the texts.

Among the rivers which take their name from the Creator is Brahmanadi, a synonym for the ancient Sarasvati, named after Brahma's wife, which has since disappeared and now flows in the substratum. The Mahabharata also mentions the river Brahmani. Then, there is the mighty Brahmaputra, which flows east from Shiva's abode at Kailash-Manasarovar. (In Tibet it is called the Tsangpo and in Bangladesh, curiously, the Yamuna which merges with the Megha and thereby takes the latter's name.) Although the Brahmaputra, literally son of Brahma, is commonly listed as one of the five male rivers of India (with Indus, Son, Gogra and Sutlej), this is a late and erroneous interpretation – the Sanskritization of the original name for this Tibeto-Burmese, Bhullambuthur (making a gurgling sound), lies at the root of this Hinduized distortion.

Brahmottara is mentioned as a *janapada* (state) in the Puranas – now identified as the western coast of the Ganga in West Bengal. Brahmapuri in the Reva district of Madhya Pradesh is now called Bahmangaon, and Brahmanvasti is now Bamanghati in the Mayurbhanj district of Orissa. Brahmagiri, in Karnataka, is best known for its Ashokan edict, but is a very ancient site with successive neolithic, chalcolithic, megalithic and Andhra-Satavahana remains.

BRAHMA'S FAMILY & ABODE

Brahma is believed to live atop Mount Mahameru, in Manovati, the centre of the nine towns which exist there. The Manusmriti (chapter 1) mentions Brahma's birth as a tale of self-emanation: "That egg was as radiant as the sun, with the colour of gold. Brahma, the great-grandfather of everything in the world, took birth by himself." This Vedantic theory of creation is an imagery which can very well be applied to the big bang theory of creation offered by modern science. The Devi Purana (*skanda* 1) gives prominence to Vishnu by making him the source of the Creator who originates in a lotus from Vishnu's navel. Brahma, through penance, acquires the ability to create from Mahavishnu and Jagadamba, and through his attribute of *rajoguna* creates the world in the colour of wood.

Here is a summary of Brahma's family tree and the events related to the Creator in various literary sources: Brahma creates daughter Sarasvati/Savitri through ejaculation in a pot after seeing the celestial nymph Urvashi. Brahma lusts after his daughter who tries to escape as a deer. In order to keep sight of her in every direction, Brahma grows four heads, Sarasvati flies upwards to hide herself, but Brahma grows a fifth head to look up. She finally succumbs as his wife. One hundred years of incest follow (Bhagavata Purana, *skanda* 11).

According to the Adiparva of the Mahabharata, Brahma has seven sons: Marichi, Angiras, Atri, Pulastya, Pulaha, Kratu and Vasishtha. These are the seven 'grand hermits'.

In Kathasaritasagara (Lavanakalambaka, *taranga* 6), Kamadeva is said to have been born from his egotism.

The Uttara Ramayana has Madhuka and Golika as the giant couple born out of Brahma's playfulness. In the Agni Purana (chapter 20), Rudra is the roaring son.

The Adi Purana (chapter 5, stanza 8) mentions Bhrigu as the hermit, while the Bhagavata Purana lists Sanaka, Sananda, Sanatana and Sanatakumara as Brahma's sons.

The 23 Prajapatis are listed as: Kashyapa, Svayambhuva Manu, Dharma, Adharma, Praheti, Heti, Vasishtha, Bhrigu, Marichi, Arishtanemi, Vivasvan, Daksha, Prachetas, Sthanu, Samshraya, Shesha, Vikrita, Kardama, Kratu, Pulaha, Pulastya, Atri, Angiras.

BRAHMA'S NAMES
From the Amarakosha, *with their meanings*

ABJAYONI lotus-born
ANDAJA born from the egg
ATMABHU born of his own accord or of the supreme spirit
BRAHMA one who increases
CHATURANANA four-faced
DHATA one who gives
DRUHINA one who hurts *asuras* (demons)
HANSAVAHANA one with the swan vehicle
HIRANYAGARBHA literally, the 'gold inside'
KAMALASANA one who sits on the lotus
LOKESHA master of the universe
NABHIJANMA born from the navel of Vishnu
PARAMESHTHIN one that stands in the highest place
PITAMAHA father
PRAJAPATI progenitor or lord of creatures
SHRASHTA one who observes
SURAJYESHTHA one who comes into being before all the *suras* (gods)
SVAYAMBHU self-born
VEDHA one who creates
VIDHATA the supreme
VIDHI one who ordains
VIRANCHI one who creates the five elements
VISHVASRIT one who creates the world

Brahma's Earthly Abode

BELOW *The Brahma* kamal, Saussurea obvallata, *which blossoms high in the arid Himalayas, is the state flower of Uttaranchal.*

ABOVE *Raja Ravi Varma of Travancore, Kerala, created a national archetype in his portraits. Here, Sarasvati, wife of Brahma, appears with a peacock which places her in Rajasthan where her husband's earthly abode lies.*

FACING PAGE *Brahma Temple at Pushkar.*

The fact that the list of pilgrimages mentioned in the Aranyakaparva of the Mahabharata begins and ends with Pushkar, is not without importance. It indicates that Brahma's pilgrimage was once considered as important as he must have been in the epic period. The Mahabharata calls Pushkar, Pitamahasarah (pond of the grandfather), using the word *pitamaha* for the revered Creator. It also mentions that praying morning and evening with Pushkar in mind "is the equivalent of bathing at all the fords... Pushkar [is] said to be the first of fords." *Tirtha*, literally a ford, metaphorically represents the 'crossing over of the worldly ocean to reach heaven'. The Pushkaramahamatya of the Padma Purana, also spares no words to list the benefits achieved by visiting Pushkar.

Then, over the years, its fame spread since the pilgrimage was open to all castes. For achieving this easy access, different castes were given various directions as points of entry to the pilgrimage. The Pushkar tradition also uses a device of proxy-pilgrimage for its popularity. A wife can pray here for her absent husband, for him to go to heaven! Even today, a group of village women can set out for Pushkar, backed by the support and trust of their men – a licensed hen party in an otherwise male-dominated society.

The Kurma Purana is most explicit in recommending Pushkar. The Kurma Purana's dates of incorporation (circa 550-750 CE, with some later additions up to 1250) point to Pushkar's period of popularity. After the Muslim invasions began, and certainly after Ajmer's Sanskrit University was destroyed in 1193 and a mosque was established there, followed by Jahangir's and Aurangzeb's heedless destruction at Pushkar, the atmosphere for worship could not have been congenial. It was long after Aurangzeb's death in 1707 and the settling of political uncertainties with the coming of the British in 1818 that the Hindu rulers took up the task of rebuilding the temples and ghats of Pushkar, reviving its popularity. After the independence of India, with the land reforms of the 1950s as well as the abolition of the privy purses in 1969, the patronage to the Brahmans declined considerably.

MATERIALISTIC FOLLOWING

The Brahma Temple in Pushkar was built by the side of the lake that is believed to have been formed by Brahma while rescuing the children of the earth from the evil demon, Vajranabha. This temple in the little town of Pushkar, in Rajasthan, is the only major thriving temple dedicated to the Creator-god in India today (see p. 186). On the other hand, temples to Vishnu, the preserver, and his many manifestations liberally dot the countryside, and together with shrines dedicated to Shiva, the regenerator, who sets into motion new cycles of creation by destroying the old, would number several hundred thousand. It is generally true that people in need or distress, do not worship as much as ask for favours from their gods: they strike secret bargains, then offer flowers to seal the deal, chant mantras, make sacrifices and grant charities in keeping with the promises made to their chosen deities. The gods, after all, are considered to be of the same mould as their devotees. If human beings can be tempted by money, why not their gods? Outside most Hindu temples, stalls sell small currency for a token fee, making it possible for even the poorest to 'bribe' their way to their desires.

However, no spiritual deals can be made at Pushkar since Brahma has completed his task of creation, giving what he can. To make demands would serve no purpose. This, perhaps, is why the Creator is the least worshipped of the Hindu trinity. After all, Vishnu preserves and sustains what we value, while if Shiva is pleased, he can delay the process of destruction and regeneration.

ABOVE *To ensure that everyone gets a share of the donations, paper currency can be exchanged for the smallest denomination of coins outside the Brahma Temple. These are distributed along the way to gods, priests, beggars, old persons and children.*

RIGHT & FACING PAGE TOP *Up a steep flight of stairs, the pilgrims actually climb the hill on which the Brahma Temple was originally built. It was subsequently added to, destroyed and rebuilt according to the changing modes of the day. The chequered court of the Brahma Temple makes a dramatic impression with its ancient stone pillars, now painted blue. The marble horse seen on the left was donated by the wife of an advocate from Surat. Although the horse has no iconographic significance, the Manusmriti narrates that the horse is sacred to Prajapati Brahma since he assumed this form when he went in search of Agni who had hidden in the waters. It is relevant to mention that even the Brahma Temple at Pushkar was destroyed by Aurangzeb. Had it not been for the private initiative of a Brahman lady from Jaipur, the Jaipur maharaja and a Maratha minister, Pushkar may well have not returned to the limelight.*

Every November, five days before the full moon of *Kartik Purnima*, the devout throng to Pushkar to wash away their sins in the magical waters of the lake. This is when Brahma is himself said to be present. They resolve then to remain as unblemished as the gods.

OTHER BRAHMA TEMPLES IN INDIA

It must not be forgotten that the heyday of Brahma was before the death of Buddha in 480 BCE, some 2,500 years ago! Broadly, Brahma was worshipped from about 600 BCE to 400 CE in the north, north-east, north-central as also in north-western India.

A few generations of neglect and lack of patronage is usually enough for a temple to be forgotten, and it is commonly, though falsely, believed that the only temple to Brahma is in Pushkar. However, if Brahma was the most important deity in the pre-Buddhist interlude to Hinduism, it is highly improbable even to consider that in the whole of India there exists only a single temple to venerate him. The sheer size of the Indian subcontinent itself defies this logic.

What did happen, though, was that in the resurgence of neo-Brahmanism during the post-Buddhist period, Brahma's importance came to be shared with Shiva and Vishnu in the composite iconography of the *trimurti*. Even though he was represented in the centre, his importance was not central in the pantheon. The more populist myths of the Shiva and Vishnu Puranas had caught the fancy of the largely illiterate populace and the intellectually-epitomized Brahma now

BELOW *The first offerings in the temple are made to a silver tortoise Kurma, embedded in the marble floor. In the myth of the 'churning of the oceans' it acted as a fulcrum.*

stood quite far removed from the lay worshippers.

In the third quarter of the 20th century, Pushkar was also 'discovered' beyond its rural Rajasthani or north-Indian pilgrims as well as cattle-fair buyers and sellers. Its rather picturesque countryside and people were to become a photographer's delight. With catalogues, books, posters and advertising campaigns, Brahma also staged a comeback with the tourists' Pushkar.

It is also observed that if Brahma had once not been so widely worshipped in Bihar – Gaya even being called the city he created – he would not have been so closely associated with the enlightenment of Buddha, nor have been incorporated into the Buddhist mythology at Nalanda and Rajgir.

JN Banerjee lists three early medieval and late Brahma shrines located at Dudahai and Khajuraho in Madhya Pradesh and at Unkal near Hubli in Karnataka. G Oppert mentions that the west-coast Tulus worship Brahmabhuta (Brahmadeva, Soma, Bharma) as a spirit which, like Brahma, has four heads, rides a *hansa*, swan, holds a water jar and rosary. Oppert's late 19th-century list includes Brahma temples in south India: Kalahasti (North Arcot district), Kutanur (near Mayavaram), Tiruvannamalai and Cebrolu (Krishna district). He also brings up Banaras where a Brahma Ghat exists. *The Bombay Gazetteer* mentions a Brahma Temple in Kolhapur. Carambolim in Goa was once a village of Brahma. Khedbrahma in Idar, Gujarat has a whole mythology related to its Brahma Temple. In Andhra, at what is now called Alampur, near Srisailam – whose greatness as a Shiva Kshetra is recorded in the 12th-century Telegu book, *Panditharadhya Charitra* by the poet Palkuriki Somanatha – lie nine Brahma temples which are unique in all of India: Bala Brahma, Kumara Brahma, Arka Brahma, Veera Brahma, Vishva Brahma, Taraka Brahma, Garuda Brahma, Svarga Brahma and Padma Brahma. The Bala Brahmeshvara Temple by the banks of the Tungabhadra is set amidst great natural beauty and is renowned for its fine sculptures.

ABOVE *When Shankaracharya expounded his understanding of Hinduism in his theory of* advaita, *he chose Brahma to represent the 'Only One' incorporating all pluralities which were, in any case, illusory. The monistic idea was not new, and as some suggest, borrowed from Islam. But it had already been enumerated in the Upanishads, composed around 400-200 BCE. When Shankara visited Pushkar in the early 9th century CE, he completed a pilgrimage dear to him, for Brahma was the ultimate principle, the final reality, the uncaused cause of his* ekam advaityam *(one essence and no other). The haloed seat where Shankaracharya sat lies venerated within the precincts of the Brahma Temple, his presence symbolized by a marble statue. The text below reads* "Shri Shri Adya Madhandya Shankracharya-ji Gaddi."

BRAHMA'S TIME CYCLE

In trying to fathom 'eternity' and applying it to the Hindu cyclic scale, the age of Brahma was evolved. In the Vishnu Purana, Brahma is said to live a hundred of his own years, each of which – *a mahayuga* – consists of 360 days and nights, equalling a thousand years of mankind. The days are called *kalpas*, and consist of 4,320 million years of mortals, during which the universe exists for four *yugas*. During his nights the universe ceases to exist, and is reproduced at the commencement of the next day or *kalpa*.

At the end of the hundred Brahma years, the life of Brahma will come to an end, and will become one with Narayana (Vishnu). Thus, thousands and thousands of Brahmas have appeared and passed away and this is a continuous process.

FACING PAGE *Garlanded with flowers and crowned impressively in silver, a life-size, four-headed Brahma seated cross-legged in* padmasana, *is the chief deity venerated at Pushkar. The idol was installed in 1727 by Maharaja Jai Singh II, the founder of Jaipur, although some attribute it to Shankaracharya, which seems rather unlikely from its iconography.*

RECORDS FROM THE REGION

Lieut. C Herbert, delt.

VIEW OF THE AJMEER LAKE WITH FORT

Lithographed by Smith, E

W. Gauci, Lithog

HILL OF TARRAGURH, FROM THE NORTH.

er & Cº Cornhill, London.

ABOVE *Brahmi on stone, circa 2nd century BCE.*

PRECEDING PAGES *A lithograph by Lt Colonel CJ Dixon of an 1850 view of Taragarh. The hill fort or* giri durg *is but one of the five types of military forts recommended in the Rigveda. The others are* jal durg *or fort protected by water;* vana durg *or forest fort;* mahi durg *or mud fort; and* dhanva durg *or desert fort.*

ABOVE *A temple at Ajaypal. Raja Ajaypal, associated with the building of Ajaymeru Durg in Ajmer at a height of over 900 metres (Rajasthan's highest fort built in 7th century CE), took solace in his old age in the sylvan solitude of the hills named after him.*

BELOW *The Pushkar inscription of Durgaraja from 925 CE, in the Government Museum, Ajmer.*

EARLY DISCOVERIES

The antiquity of the region of Pushkar and its environs goes back to several millennia. Archaeological evidence, as Bridget and Raymond Allchin write, would suggest that habitation may not have been possible up to the end of the Pleistocene phase (starting circa 1.65 million years ago), but there is evidence of the existence of the upper paleolithic (circa 20,000 BCE and later) and mesolithic cultures (8000-2000 BCE) in the immediate vicinity of Pushkar. With its good supply of fresh water, Pushkar saw the development of microlithic sites which were primarily living or camping sites. Pottery of the chalcolithic period (dating back to 2nd-1st millennium BCE) has been discovered at several of these sites. One particular site has yielded a copper fish-hook. Such evidence points to Pushkar being an inhabited region from prehistoric times, perhaps from the paleolithic age – if not earlier.

Moving further down in time to the historical period, in the Government Museum of Ajmer, housed in Akbar's Daulat Khana fort-palace, lie many a silent stone. One among them is particularly significant, for it is considered to be among the earliest epigraphical records found within the borders of India. Excavated at Badli near Vijaynagar, reached via Gulabpura from Ajmer, the find is ascribed to the 2nd century BCE. The fragmentary inscription on buff-pink stone is in the Mauryan Brahmi script and may be tentatively read in four lines as *ra_a_ _/ ra ta ra ta va/_ma ha ra / tha ma ra ma ra*. The language has been identified as Prakrit. Literally, Prakrit is derived from *prakriti*, or nature, and simply means natural. It has been broadly applied to many proto-Indo-Aryan vernaculars. The fact that it is not carved on a flat slab but on a faceted, pillar-like stone suggests that it may well have been a *kirti-sthambha,* or a tower of victory, recording the name of a builder. Or it may be a pillar fragment – like the pillars of the near-contemporary Mauryan emperor, Ashoka (r. 273-232 BCE). Prakrit was the language of the masses. The Prakrit spoken and written in this area was probably Saurashtri, which intermixed with Scythian dialects to become the mother of Gurjari – the old Gujarati which gave birth to modern Gujarati, Marwari and Rajasthani.

One of the earliest *shivalingas* found in Rajasthan was discovered on the pilgrimage routes of Pushkar (for details of the route, see p. 59). It is as tall as a human and its iconography as astonishing as it is impressive. Highlighting the Lakulisha aspect of Shiva meditating with an erection (*urdhvalinga tapasya*), it has images of Krishna, Balarama, Devi and even Surya – perhaps suggesting their composite form compressed into a *linga* representing Shiva.

This unique and amazing *shivalinga* is contemporary with Lakulisha (circa 200 CE), who is considered the original teacher of this cult related to one of the oldest forms of Shiva as Pashupati (as in the horned 'ascetic' of the Indus Valley seal which dates back to circa 2800-1900 BCE). The four disciples of Lakulisha lived and preached in Rajasthan and Gujarat. Lakulisha (literally meaning *isha* or lord with a *lakula* or club) and the ithyphallic resemblance to *urdhvalinga tapasya* gave this cult its symbol and name, as well as its final reputation for depravity.

This cult began with simple austerities and asceticism, chanting '*om*' while meditating and vowing to shed greed and anger. However, by the 12th century, activities such as orgies with loud bell sounds, sorcery using human skulls as drinking bowls and smearing bodies with ash from cremation grounds had marginalized them completely. Their schools too had become dens of vice and promiscuity.

Some 'left-handed' sects who succeeded them are the Kapalikas, *kanphata*–Gorakhnathis (who also have a seat at Pushkar) and the Aghoris who can still be found in Banaras.

The presence of a handful of practitioners of these sects did in no way suggest the depravity of all of Hindu society, nor of its dharma. On the contrary, it was a pointer to the limits of

ABOVE *Four-sided* shivalinga, *9th century CE with seated Brahma (seen above), Vishnu, Shiva and Surya.*

LEFT *The anthropomorphic* chaturmukha shivalinga *with representations of deities from the 2nd century CE. The images were defaced by the Muslim armies, but its size (around 2 metres) reveals that it must have been housed in an impressive temple.*

BELOW A shivalinga *from the 10th century CE, with Brahma, Vishnu, Shiva and Surya standing on its four sides. Both* shivalingas *(left & below) are from Kama in Bharatpur and were found in the countryside. The temples that once housed them were destroyed by Aurangzeb in the late 17th century and in the late 19th century the images reached the Government Museum, Ajmer.*

AN HISTORICAL OVERVIEW OF AJMER

RULER	DATE	NO. OF YEARS
Pratiharas of Mandor (Marwar)	6th century at Naran & Shakambhari[1]	
Chauhans of Ajmer	700–1192	492
Sultan of Ghori	1192–93	1
Chauhans of Ajmer	1194–95	1
Sultans of Delhi	1195–1400	205
Sisodias of Mewar	1400–1455	55
Sultans of Mandu	1455–1505	50
Sisodias of Mewar	1505–1533	28
Sultans of Gujarat	1534–1535	1
Rathors of Marwar	1535–1556	21
Mughal Emperors	1556–1719	163
Rathors of Marwar	1719–21	2
Mughal Kings of Delhi	1722–43	21
Rathors of Marwar	1743–56	13
Ram Singh of Marwar & Scindias of Gwalior	1756–58	2
Scindias of Gwalior[2]	1758–87	29
Rathors of Marwar	1787–91	4
Scindias of Gwalior[3]	1791–1818	27
British Government	1818-1947	129

1 In the 7th century, when Hiuen Tsang visited India, the peninsula of Gujarat was known as Saurashtra. Marwar, the current-day Jodhpur region, was then called Gurjara. How, in the course of their migrations, that the Gurjaras came to pass through the Pushkar area, which is bordered by the great sandy plains of Marwar, is not improbable or difficult to imagine. Cunningham's *Ancient Geography of India* also states that the Gurjara people once dwelt in the Punjab and subsequently migrated to the Kathiawar peninsula and adjoining regions. Interestingly, in 1000 CE, Rajyapala headed the Gurjara Pratiharas from Kanyakubja (Kanauj) from where the Rathors had come to Marwar in the 7th century. Gujranwala in the Punjab may well have been an original seat of the Gurjaras. As late as 1761, Charat Singh, grandfather of Ranjit Singh, realized its importance and established his stronghold at Gujranwala where in the following year he was unsuccessfully challenged by the Mughal governor of Lahore.

2 Part of the Ajmer district remained under the Rathors till 1791.

3 The Rathors remained in possession of a part of the district of Ajmer from 1803 to 1806.

ABOVE *A 19th-century painting from Jodhpur of Prithviraj Chauhan III hunting tiger, probably in the vicinity of Ajmer.*

FACING PAGE TOP *On the hills above the defile in Nagpahar, which brings the road from Ajmer to Pushkar, lies Lakshmi Pol attributed to Prithviraj Chauhan III. The unfinished fort can also be seen in the distance. Legend has it that whatever was built by day was demolished by the spirits in the night. Even today, the hilltop is strewn with large, slim bricks which are considered auspicious when beginning the construction of a house. The Gurjaras are entrusted with this task and they charge Rs 250 to bring down one symbolic brick, seen here in the foreground.*

freedom to which some people could take their austerities or licentiousness. However, international travellers remained fascinated with such sects, and their representations and descriptions went a long way in positioning India in the minds of their countrymen as a land of bizarre and occult practices. Meanwhile, both the high end of evolved Hindu thought and its quiet, mainstream practices went unrecorded.

AJMER & PUSHKAR

Writing in the early 1940s, historian Har Bilas Sarda describes Ajmer as an important destination in the agenda for political supremacy in India between the 12th and the 19th centuries. Sarda also quotes the *Chambers' Encyclopaedia* which carries the same thought: "The history of Ajmer is the epitome of the history of India, just as India is the epitome of the world."

Not much is known of the rulers of the area until the arrival of the Chauhans. Although the Chauhans ruled from the salt-lake city of Sambhar, and had long held this region as their territory, it was only in the 7th century that the Ajaymeru Durg was raised on an invincible vantage point with long, vigilant views over the landscape. There are three varying accounts of Ajmer's antiquity, all attributing its foundation to the Chauhan kings. The first account attributes it to Ajayraj or Ajaypal Chahaman (Chauhan) (r. 1108-23); the second (*Prithviraj-vijay*) to Ajaydeva (r. 1123-50); and the third (Chand Bardoi's *Prithviraj-raso*) to Ajaydeva's son Ajaji (r.1150-53).

The tale of internal dissentions and fraternal treachery is not new to the history of any land, and especially not to the story of Raja Prithviraj Chauhan (r. 1153–92), who when faced with the forces of Muhammad of Ghori, was "seven times captured [by] the Sultan and seven times released [by] him" (as Colonel James Tod wrote). On the first occasion that the Sultan could capture Prithviraj, Ghori blinded him and then after humiliating him, killed him with his sword. This marked the beginning of Muslim rule in northern India, which then continued for centuries in some regional context or the other. Percival Spear writes that after the Battle of Tarain when Muhammad of Ghori blinded and executed Prithviraj Chauhan, "the Hindus were frankly a subject people". But the Battle of Tarain was to teach the Hindus that war was war and that there were no losers in history.

BELOW *Ruins of Lakshmi Pol on a site abandoned by Prithviraj Chauhan. A Lakshmi Pol also exists at Taragarh, on the outermost line of fortifications, on the way when one arrives from Inderkot, past the wells of Kela Bai and Amba Bai.*

THE ANTIQUITY OF PUSHKAR

Archaeological evidence shows that Pushkar is much older than Ajmer, and was possibly a settlement even in the prehistoric period. The literary and historical evidence further reveals:

The Ramayana mentions that the sage Vishvamitra performed *tapa* (penance) at Pushkar (*sarga* 62, *shloka* 28). It refers again to Pushkar saying that the celestial enchantress, Menaka came to bathe in its waters (*sarga* 63, *shloka* 15).

In the Mahabharata, Pushkar is not only taken as a starting point for a grand pilgrimage of the entire country, but its merit is again repeated at the end of the dialogue on pilgrimages, where the 88 *tirthas* end with Prayag. It also advises Yudhishthira to bathe in Pushkar after entering the jungles of Sindh and crossing the small rivers.

The earliest punch-marked coins, anterior to the 4th century BCE, have been found in Pushkar's environs, along with Bactrian, Greek, Kshatrapa, Gupta, Gadhaiya and Mughal coins, and the issues of the rulers Samantadeva, Ajaydeva and his queen Somaladevi, Someshvara and Prithviraj. This would suggest that the region was an important centre through the ages.

Stone inscriptions dated to the 2nd century BCE from the Sanchi Stupa near Bhopal mention charitable donations made by the Buddhist monks, or *bhikshus*, Arhadina, Nagarakshita, Arya, Buddharakshita, Himgiri, Pusak and Isidata – all inhabitants of Pushkar.

In 1878, Louis Rousselet had noted, "The crest of the mountain consists of a perpendicular wall, sixty feet in breadth, through which runs the road, originally a natural fissure in the rock, enlarged for this purpose. Before entering this narrow passage, we took a farewell look at Ajmer, whose houses and gardens covered the opposite bank of the lake, rising one above the other like an amphitheatre on the slopes of the beautiful Teraghur."

In 1955, Jack Gibson, who was the legendary principal of Mayo College, Ajmer, for over three decades (1937-1969), recorded that "Pushkar is the other side of a little pass from which you have views of the desert in front and Ajmer behind, and the road, all the way, was full of peasants on foot, animals, and every sort of conveyance: buses, tongas, bullock wagons and ancient cars dug out for the occasion. We passed a dead pony and smashed tonga and a bus upside down, but arrived safely to a most picturesque outing. The people in this part of India are both better looking and more colourfully dressed than in the U.P."

BELOW *A lithograph of the marble pavilions by CW Waddington. Today, only two of the five marble pavilions erected near the Ana Sagar lake by Shah Jahan remain. The northernmost of these was removed in the early 19th century by a Maratha governor and put atop Akbar's Daulat Khana fort, south of the western bastion, to be used as a temple.*

THE IMPORTANCE OF GURJARAS/GURJARA-PRATIHARAS

During the early part of the second century CE, a tribe known as the Uttamabhadras were ruling the Pushkar-Ajmer region. They were subordinate allies of Nahapana, a Shaka (Scythian) ruler of the Deccan. In a Nasik inscription, one Ushavadata, a son-in-law of Nahapana, claims to have gone to 'Pushkara' for ceremonial consecration after inflicting a crushing defeat on the Malavas who were posing a threat to his allies, the Uttamabhadras.

As the Shaka power was eclipsed soon after by the Satavahanas of the Deccan, the Pushkar-Ajmer area would have been dominated either by the powerful Malava republic or their neighbours, the Arjunayanas of the Jaipur region. Both of them, along with many others were subdued by the imperial Guptas during the 4th century.

With the decline of the Guptas, a dynasty known to history as the Pratiharas of Mandor (Jodhpur) rose to prominence in Rajasthan about the middle of the sixth century CE. Soon they extended their power to Ujjain and then to Kanauj, which became the capital city of the extensive Pratihara empire that included the greater part of northern India. They finally succumbed to the forces of Mahmud of Ghazni. The Pratiharas had played a very important role in checking the advance of the Arabs into India beyond the Sindh-Multan region.

Nagabhata I, the founder of the imperial Pratihara line of Ujjain and Kanauj is glorified in the Gwalior inscription of his descendant Bhoja as '*pratihara*', for having crushed the large armies of the powerful Baluchis and Arabs (called *mlechhas* in this inscription). His successors too, proved a strong bulwark against Arab invaders as noted by the Arab writers Sulaiman (851 CE) and Al-Masudi (915-916 CE).

The various Pratihara kings have been referred to as Gurjaresha, Ghurjararaja or simply as Gurjara in the inscriptions of their contemporary rulers. But the Pratiharas of Mandor or Kanauj do not call themselves Gurjaras. Instead, they trace their descent rather incongruously, from both, a Brahman called Harichandra and from Lakshmana who is said to have acquired the epithet Pratihara (door-keeper) by acting as a sentry for his elder brother Rama during their battle against Meghanada – the latter being described as the 'humbler' of the pride of Indra. It is possible that the Pratiharas were a clan of the Gurjara tribe that possibly entered India from the north-west during the early centuries of the Common Era. They would then have invented a genealogy for themselves to claim a Kshatriya status, as did many other Rajput clans of foreign or indigenous origin. However, the claims of the Gurjaras or Gurjars of today to a Pratihara descent are not based on a living tradition. Nor is it certain that all the communities known as Gujars have a single ethnic identity. The Gujar claims to a Pratihara connection are a part of the recent rather curious phenomenon of numerous Indian communities from Agarwals to Gujars seeking glory by inventing royal lineages in a society governed by a constitution which abolished monarchy and seeks to level all social-political hierarchies!

RIGHT *Outside and inside views of one of the relocated marble* baradaris, *which now sits on the southern* burj *of the Daulat Khana palace of Akbar. It housed a temple of Lakshmi Narayan in the Sepoy Mutiny of 1857 when the Europeans locked themselves in Akbar's palace and fortified it with cannons on the bastions. The idol in the temple could not be worshipped and was installed in the Lakshmi Kant Temple near Agra Gate of Ajmer.*

In the layering of the history of Rajasthan, and particularly in its reinterpretation by Colonel James Tod (who wrote his *Annals and Antiquities of Rajasthan* at the instance of the East India Company and to the glory of the reigning Rajput dynasties of the time, with whom they had signed treaties of subordinate alliance), many distortions and inventions

could only be expected. Later historians have pointed out that Tod relied on bardic legends and court historians rather than epigraphic, numismatic and other more reliable sources of history, many of which were unearthed after his time.

By a long oral tradition, even today it is said that in Pushkar the bathing ghats were first made around the 7th century CE by Nahar Mal Rao Pratihara or Parihara of Mandor (near Jodhpur) of the Gurjara-Pratihara line. There are also legends of a Gurjara king, Nagabhata who constructed several stepwells and supposedly grazed 900 thousand cows in the area! Historically, these oral remnants can be easily connected to the Gurjara-Pratihara king Nagabhata I (r. 724-760 CE). He was variously known as Nagavoloka, Nahar Dev Nagabhata or simply Gurjareshvar Nahar Rai. The Puranas also mention Nagabhata I as the founder of the pilgrimage of Pushkar. In all probability, the Nagpahar is also named after Nagabhata I.

The Gurjaras still come in large numbers on *Baisakhi Purnima* (April-May) for *pinda-daan* ceremonies to honour their ancestors with 12-hour rites followed by a *malpua* and dal feast. This pilgrimage seems to have maintained its own identity – away from the *Sharad Purnima* (October-November) celebrations, now a major tourist jamboree.

It is said that the Mandor raja, who constructed the first ghat at Pushkar, was a Gurjara-Pratihara. Later, when the Rathors ruled Marwar from Mandor-Jodhpur, the Gurjara Ghat lost its name and importance. It was only in the late 20th century that the Gurjara community bought over the Sikar Ghat of the Raja of Shekhavati, when his widow migrated to her homeland in Nepal after his death.

Now the Gurjaras have their own ghat after centuries. Besides the fact that Brahma chose a Gurjara to be his second bride, and the location of two Gurjara *dharamshalas* close to the Brahma Temple, another piece of evidence which determines their importance in the historic link (besides their historical kingdoms of Mandor, Naran, Shakhambhari and Nadol which are in the vicinity of Pushkar) is the presence of three Gurjara temples at Pushkar: Devanarayan Temple, Bhuna-ji ka Dev at Gurjara Ghat, and the Bhojraj Temple close behind the Brahma Temple itself.

ABOVE *The impressive Ajaymeru Durg – later Garh Beethli and Taragarh of the Chauhans – crowns the skyline over Ajmer. Its 6-metre thick fortifications were built on the edge of precipices making it inaccessible. Only the south was prone to attack, so sturdy bastions interspersed the battlements at short distances.*

Much ambiguity remains about the early Gurjara-Pratiharas – whether the Gurjaras were the rulers or the ruled. The Report on the Census of 1891, published in 1894 mentions that "the Pushkarna-Brahmans form one of the subdivisions of the Gurjars, the fifth tribe of the Punch-Deravar Brahmans", finding yet another link between the Gurjaras and Pushkar. While many early dynasties were Brahmans – Shungas, Kanvas, Satvahanas, Vakatakas – many yearned for martial Rajput status as rulers, which was actually one step down in the cast hierarchy. These include the Chauhans, Pratiharas, Chalukyas, Gohilas/Sisodias whose early inscriptions claim their Brahman origins.

THE PILGRIMAGE

ABOVE *Before arriving in Ajmer, modern signage now directs visitors to Pushkar so that they may bypass the crowded city.*

PRECEDING PAGES *On Saptarishi Ghat, a tree along the pilgrimage route becomes an object of worship and veneration.*

BELOW *Farmers who walk to Pushkar, taking their pilgrimage seriously, and others who see in it a form of penance for their worldly sins – even measuring the road by laying their bodies on it – need to stop frequently. Roadside tea shops spring up during the fair, offering a quick* kullar *of tea in a terracotta cup, easily dispensed and ecologically bio-degradable. And yet, plastics have begun to litter the routes which are dirtied faster than they can be cleaned.*

THE IMPORTANCE OF TIRTHAGURU PUSHKAR

Within the long sojourn on earth, mundane human chores and preoccupations seem to sully the soul. A visit to a *tirtha*, or a place of pilgrimage, serves the purpose of a cleansing journey. Usually, a *tirtha* is a place made sacred by miracles, or by man's desire to be at a beautiful natural spot – be it a mountain, a forest, a river or a lake.

The sacred lake at Pushkar is considered by Hindus to be among the holiest waters along with the much less accessible Manasarovar situated at 4,560 metres en route to Mount Kailash in Tibet, where Shiva supposedly resides.

What are the criteria which have earned Pushkar the epithets of *tirthaguru* (guru of pilgrim sites) and *tirtharaj* (king of pilgrim places)?

According to the Puranas, the 18 compilations of Brahmanical mythological lore, there are four categories of pilgrimages for Hindus. In a hierarchy of descending order, these are: *daiva-tirthas*, created by the gods, mainly by the male deities of the trinity – Brahma, Vishnu and Shiva; *asura-tirthas*, associated with the destruction of demons by the trinity; *arsha-tirthas*, related with the austerities, penances and sacrifices of renowned seers and sages; and *manusha-tirthas*, holy places created by men – preferably the rulers of the solar and lunar dynasties.

Rated on these criteria, Pushkar stands unique and highest among pilgrimages because it qualifies on all four grounds. First, it was chosen by Brahma while both Vishnu and Shiva attended the sacrificial fire rite that he held for its creation. Second, the demon Vajranabha, who performed penance in the Meru valley to propitiate Brahma, was destroyed here by Pradyumna, the son of Krishna. Shiva also took the form of a goat to kill the demon Vashkali here. Third, the sages Agastya, Bhartrihari, Kanva/Kashyapa, Jamadagni, Vamadeva, Vishvamitra, Kapila, Markandeya, Pulastya and even Yama, the lord of death, are believed to have done penance in caves here. Fourth, the Pratiharas of Mandor, the Kachhawahas of Amber/Jaipur, the Hadas of Kotah and Bundi, the Rathors of Marwar/Jodhpur, the Sisodias of Mewar/Udaipur and the Marathas of Gwalior have all had a hand in building and repairing temples and ghats at Pushkar.

As a pristine oasis in the Thar desert, Pushkar must always have appealed to the weary traveller or warrior and once the legendary Sarasvati river also flowed here. The sanctity and necessity of flowing water can hardly be overemphasized because the Ganga basin figures most prominently in all the *tirtha* lists of the epics and holy scriptures: *"Pushkaradhipati tirthani gangadhayasaritasthata"* (Pushkar occupies the highest place among pilgrim sites as does the sacred Ganga among rivers).

The myths related to Brahma and the creation of Sarasvati have already been examined in the preceding chapter and this is in keeping with the association of the birth of sacred rivers with major gods of Hinduism. Shiva is linked with the birth of the Ganga and the Narmada, and Vishnu's acts relate with first releasing the waters of the Ganga to flow into the *kamandala*, the ascetic's pot, which

LEFT *Nine kilometres before Pushkar, travellers profit from the shade of the trees at Hokra village as they smoke the hookah and join fellow Rajasthanis in a game of* chaupad*, likened to the Chinese ludo.*

LEFT *Two kilometres from Pushkar, to make the entry auspicious for pilgrims, a row of* neem *and* peepal *trees have been entwined to grow together. The* neem *(Margosa) is symbolic of Narayana (Vishnu), while the* peepal *or* ashvattha *(*Ficus indica*) also called* peepli*, is symbolic of Lakshmi, and they are thus married. Buddha attained enlightenment under the* peepal*, and it is mentioned in sacred writings as a cosmological tree which has its roots in heaven and branches on earth.*

Brahma carries. The presence of the Sarasvati at Pushkar is also attributed to a Vishnu legend. It was he who asked the river to flow this way to put off the fires of the great *yajna* of Brahma.

With such a strong mythological lineage, Pushkar is destined to remain on the top of the list of Hindu pilgrimages, despite the vanishing act of the Sarasvati river. However, one lull in the popularity of Pushkar is recorded in history. After the destruction and conquest of Ajmer at the end of the 12th century by Muhammad of Ghori, people lived in fear and insecurity. Conspicuous patronage, building activity and worship at Pushkar was revived and thrived only in the 18th century. After 1947 – and particularly after the privy purses were abolished – royal patronage has waned, and now the priests rely more on the largesse of common pilgrims.

ABOVE *Ajgandh Mahadev at Ajaypal where the* linga *smells of* aj, *or a goat.*

BELOW *This is where Ajaypal, the founder of Ajmer, retired in his old age and worshipped. In a forlorn, rocky valley of the Aravallis, an ancient well with circular steps still testifies to the age-old importance of water in this region.*

PUSHKAR'S BOUNDLESS SCALE

> *Ask a Hindu about his god, or what he calls his relationship to his god, and you would encounter a very confused and disturbed person. If he is cajoled to answer he may hesitatingly offer to describe it as bhakti [devotion], sakhya [friendship], prem [love] and in a lot more ways leaving a very confused questioner. The reason is simple: he does not have a 'religion'. He has his dharma which defines more than his god.... Although Hindus hold their deities in veneration, most of them desire to ultimately free themselves of the bondage of every deity and every god and roam free in a realm of the pure and blissful spirit.*
>
> — SHASHI S SHARMA, *Oh My God*

The open, nebulous approach to prayer as a way of life, a continuous conduct of personal and public piety, is what keeps open the parameters of the dharma which is Hinduism. If a temple is made for the purpose of personal worship and self-cleansing of some Hindus, it is not to suggest that for the others the trees outside, the rocks, the springs, the stars, the wind and all its directions, are not venerable enough for worship. For Hindus, God is everywhere – possibly explaining the scale at which the pilgrimage of Pushkar has been conceived and laid.

The Hindus have always been aware that within their much-maligned but 'democratic' choice of 33 million gods, and despite being called polytheistic in a rather derogatory and condescending hierarchy – they have only one God.

The Pushkar *kshetra*, or the region of the pilgrimage, is roughly 4 x 9 kilometres. Walking in the vast wilderness of the billion-year-old Aravallis, pilgrims can sense the raw energy of the planet-forming processes. At the foot of a mountain, pilgrims are reminded of the reality beyond Pushkar – of Rajasthan and of India. Then, as one rises with the vast consciousness of space – of Asia, the hemispheres, our explored and mapped planet, to some of the fathomed mysteries of our solar system – one may finally conceive the universe as "that sea of ignorance beyond the fringes of human knowledge" which even Einstein called God.

The wise Adi Shankaracharya, who, faced with the philosophical challenges of Buddhism propounded the monistic philosophy of *advaita*, is supposed to have craved pardon on his death bed for three sins. The honesty of these submissions is particularly telling in this context. Walker notes that the Shankaracharya asked to be forgiven "for confining Him who is without Form, to stone and mortar; for describing Him, who transcends all qualities; and for having frequented temples, since by doing so he had denied the omnipresence of His divinity."

ABOVE *This androgynous image of Shiva Ardhanarishvara is popularly worshipped at Ajaypal as the* 'roothi rani', *the queen who is angry, showing how little classical iconography touches the devotees.*

THE SARASVATI RIVER: GEOLOGY, MYTHOLOGY & HISTORY

The lake at Pushkar is also called Sarasvata, perhaps after the Sarasvati which once flowed here. Other Sarasvatis flow in eastern Afghanistan, Rajgir in Magadha (Patna) and Raunakshi in

Devotees are as happy worshipping anthropomorphic images (above) as also this aniconic form (right inset) in the other shrine at Ajaypal.
"I dive into the sea of forms (rupa) *hoping that I may come upon the gem of the formless* (arupa, *the absolute Brahman)."*
— RABINDRANATH TAGORE

ABOVE *A cow grazes at Kakreshvar, near the* sangam *of the three rivers Nanda-Prachi-Sarasvati. In the Puranas, the underground Sarasvati is called Antah Salila, the one with a subterranean flow. The Padma Purana details the legend of this confluence with a cow-lion tale in its Shrishti Khanda. The cow Nandini was grazing in this area when a lion caught her. "My calf is hungry at home. Can I feed it and return for you to eat me?" Nandini pleaded. Reluctantly, the lion conceded to her incredulous appeal and let her go. Soon the cow and calf returned, both pleading to be eaten by the lion. Seeing this display of the cow's word of honour, the lion recalled his previous life when he was Raja Prabhanjan – and with this awareness, his curse was lifted and he went to heaven. Nandini flows from Makrol Mata and the underground Sarasvati flows from Prayag, past Pushkar. The three meet at Bhaunath near Pisangan, merge with the Sagarmati, become the Luni, and flow into the Rann of Kutch. A project to make the shy, underground Sarasvati river reappear on the surface is now underway and may eventually become a reality someday. It is near here that the most ancient and impressive figurative* shivalinga *of Rajasthan, dating to the 2nd century CE, was found and is now protected on site by the Archaeological Survey of India* (*see p. 25*).

BELOW *This* linga *of Chandrashekhar Mahadev, from the destroyed Sanskrit University of Vishal Deva in Ajmer, is now installed in the courtyard of Kakreshvar Mahadev near Nand village.*

Gujarat. But the one at Pushkar originates in the hills of Sirmur, emerges in the plains at Adi Badri, and disappears in the sands at Chamasodbheda, called Vinashana in the Mahabharata. The Saraswat Brahmans of the north-west, considered the purest of their caste, are named after the Sarasvati river. The Sarasvati which disappeared at Vinashana, near Kurukshetra, is believed to have reappeared at Pushkar in five streams to increase its sanctity.

Remote sensing matched with a vast storehouse of ancient legends, have now concretely tracked the course of the Sarasvati river which disappeared into the substrata, some 4,000 years ago. The historical evidence relating to Pushkar takes it back only to 400 BCE. But that the pilgrimage site of Pushkar is at least as old as the vanished Sarasvati, which used to flow not far from the Pushkar lake, can be ascertained with the symbolisms of the myth of Brahma's daughter/wife Savitri – also called Sarasvati. Legend interpreted that she disappeared in the form of a deer when her father lusted after her. Today, the stagnant Sarasvati water that has been drilled on the Indo-Pakistan border, has been dated back to 4,000 years.

Also, a parallel oral myth seems to have been transferred downstream from Prayag – now Allahabad, where the invisible Sarasvati's meeting with the Ganga and the Yamuna at the sacred *sangam*, or confluence, is considered most auspicious by Hindus. While the Ganga and Yamuna flowed east into the Bay of Bengal, the Sarasvati flowed west through Rajasthan into the Rann of Kutch. It is still believed that the Sarasvati flows and invisibly first meets the two major northern rivers at Allahabad. Later, downstream in the invisible Sarasvati's flow, another *sangam* is believed to happen, about 6 kilometres from Pushkar, at the foot of the Nand Parvat, where the Nanda-Prachi-Sarasvati are supposed to meet. This is the lesser-known of the two *sangams*, but pilgrims circumambulating Pushkar still visit this site near Kakreshvar-Makreshvar.

According to the findings of geologists, the slow tectonic movements on the Indian subcontinent from Pakistan to Assam began some 1.7 million years ago in the Pleistocene period in the Siwalik Hills of the Sirmur region. Writes Saswati Paik, by "the late Pleistocene glaciation, the climate became warmer, the glaciers began to break up and the frozen water held by them surged forth in great floods, inundating the alluvial plains in front of the mountains." In the Rigveda, these are the Sapta Sindhu, the seven mighty water channels. Of these, the only two major rivers that flowed from the mountains into the sea, were the Sarasvati and the Sindhu or Indus which gave India its name. "The hymns in praise of the Sarasvati are probably some of the oldest, composed more than 8000 years ago," writes Paik. But when

a major avalanche blocked the supply of glacial melt to the Sarasvati, its flow became non-perennial. Its wide channel-bed flowed only in the monsoons. And it became from a wide, life-giving reality into one with a mythical flow.

West of Mount Kailash in Tibet, lies Kapala-tirtha where the Sarasvati first originated. It still flows out south of the Mana pass and meets the Alakananda, 3 kilometres south of Mana village. It used to flow south-west via Adibadri, Bhavanipur and Balchapur in Uttaranchal through Punjab and Rajasthan, into the Great Rann of Kutch in Gujarat. The changed courses of the river and millennia of accumulated silt may have dried the full flow of the Sarasvati, but geomorphic features like its 3-kilometre wide bed were responsible for drawing the attention of a British engineer. CF Oldham was riding a horse in 1893 along the tiny trickle of the Ghaggar, which seemed totally incongruous with its rather wide sand bed. Intrigued, he had wondered if that was not where the missing Sarasvati once flowed. The Remote Sensing Services Centre in Jodhpur has now mapped its width to be as much as 8 kilometres wide in certain places. Over 1,000 ancient archaeological sites have also been found along its banks and these date back to 3000 BCE. Someday, excavations on the peripheries of Pushkar – particularly around Burha Pushkar – may unfold older layers of history. In Rajasthan, the Sarasvati has appropriately conformed to its name because in its hydro-geological evolution it lived out its last stages in stagnant lakes and pools.

ABOVE *Sarasvati, the wife of Brahma, depicted in a late 19th-century oleograph as the goddess of learning and the arts. She is shown playing a veena and holding a palm-leaf manuscript.*

BELOW *This view shot from Nandrai Mata, atop the hill behind the village of Nand, shows the southern ranges which ring-in Pushkar. The central dry belt, beyond the cultivated green fields, is where the legendary Sarasvati river once flowed from left to right. Below the small white temple* shikhar *seen in the distance, mid-right, is the* sangam *of the three rivers Nanda-Prachi-Sarasvati.*

The east-west axis is not perpendicular to the north-south, as these directions are naturally protected by the high Aravalli ranges.

East: Within Pushkar

Atmateshvar Mahadev

South-west: Ajaypal

Ajgandh Mahadev

West: Near Nand village

Kakreshvar Mahadev

Makreshvar Mahadev

SHIVA AS CHATURDIKALOKAPALA: GUARDIAN OF THE FOUR DIRECTIONS

When Brahma held his *yajna* at Pushkar, away from the menacing Kali in the skies, he created four *shivalingas* and asked Shiva to guard his fire rites from the four directions. As *lokapalas*, or guarding deities, four protective *shivalingas* still stand, reminders of Shiva's role as 'place guard'.

If Brahma was installing himself at Pushkar in the Vedic times, his choice of Shiva for protecting the four directions is not unusual, because Shiva was only a minor deity at that time. Indra, Varuna, Kubera and Yama were more important deities of the Vedic age. It was by the Gupta period (4th century CE) that these Vedic gods of import were reduced to the status of *lokapalas*, and by the time of the Agamas, Shiva and Vishnu had became prominent gods in the Hindu pantheon.

This also connects with the legends of two early temples of Pushkar – the Kapaleshvar and the Atmateshvar. The duty of a *pala*, or a guardian, was possibly delegated to Shiva because Brahma did not choose to invite him for his *yajna* since he held one of Brahma's skulls in his hand (see p. 12). This is why Shiva – or at his instigation, a naked man, Atmat – is supposed to have upset the fire rite by throwing a skull, the removal of which produced two more, then four and so on, till he had to be appeased. The site of this incident is the Kapaleshvar Temple, while the Atmateshvar *shivalinga* was installed to please Shiva so that he would not continue to wreck up the fire rite.

Besides Pushkar, Brahma is also mentioned (in the Matsya and Kurma Puranas, and in an inscription of Vishvarupasena) as having performed sacrifices on the banks of the *triveni* at Prayag.

North-east: Vaidyanath

Vaidyanath Mahadev

ASHTADIKAPALA: GUARDIANS OF THE EIGHT DIRECTIONS

Directions orient our planet with the cosmos through their relation with the sun. The worshipper normally faces east, and then moves clockwise, so that the other directions appear and offer their blessings.

A popular version about Nagpahar disregards the historical king Nagabhata I and takes the tale back to the Brahma's mythical fire sacrifice on the 13th day. The sacrifice was disturbed by Bhattu Brahman, who let loose a snake among the Brahmans. The reptile coiled itself round Bhrigu Rishi whose son invoked a curse against Bhattu that he might become a snake. Bhattu went to his grandfather Brahma who consoled him that he would find the ninth order of snakes at Nagpahar. Withdrawing there, he received worship on the fifth day of the dark half of Sawan, at a tank called Nagkund.

The elephant guardians mentioned below are also spoken of in the Padma Purana. The other direction-related associations are listed in the chart below:

RIGHT *A 19th-century photo-lithograph by W Griggs of a carved stone ceiling from Ganjigatti, Dharwar district, representing the regents of the eight points of the compass.*

NAME	SYNONYM	ASSOCIATED RIVERS/WATERS	ATTRIBUTES
Jyeshtha Pushkar also Vriddha/Burha	Brahma Pushkar	Suprabha	*Rajoguna* (Creative activity, expansion or motion)
Madhya Pushkar	Vishnu Pushkar	Chandra/Shuddha Vapi	*Sattvaguna* (Goodness)
Kanishtha Pushkar	Rudra Pushkar	Kanak, Nanda, Prachi	*Tamoguna* (Darkness)

The fact that Rudra-Shiva should be the presiding deity of the main Pushkar is attributed to the fact that the small island on the lake which is considered the *yagna sthala* of Brahma has a temple to Shiva. From *Kartik Shukla Paksha Ekadashi* till *Purnima*, a *yajna* is still held on the island to honour Rudra-Shiva.

	DIRECTION	GUARDIAN DEITY	ELEPHANT GUARDIAN & SPOUSE	SNAKE GUARDIAN	WEAPON	COLOUR	CASTE	SHIVA AS LOKAPALA
1	East	Indra	Airavata-Abhramu	Ananta	*Vajra* (Thunderbolt)	Red	Kshatriya	Atmateshvar Mahadev
2	South-East	Agni	Pundarika-Kapila	Abhoga	*Shakit* (Spear)	Red	Kshatriya	
3	South	Yama	Vamana-Pingala	Padmaka	*Danda* (Rod)	Orange	Vaishya	
4*	South-West	Nirriti	Kumuda-Anupama	Shankhapala	*Kunta* (Lance)	Yellow	Vaishya	Ajgandh Mahadev
5	West	Varuna	Anjan-Anjana	Varuna	*Pasha* (Noose)	Black	Shudra	Kakreshvar-Makreshvar
6	North-West	Vayu	Pushpadanta-Subhadanti	Kulika	*Dhvaja* (Pole)	Blue	Shudra	
7	North	Kubera	Sarvabhauma-Tamrakarni	Vasuki	*Khadga* (Broad dagger)	Pink	Brahman	
8*	North-East	Ishana	Supratika-Anjanavati	Mahapadma	*Trishula* (Trident)	Grey or White	Brahman	Vaidyanath Mahadev

* The four cardinal directions do not seem to have been followed for Pushkar, perhaps because of the mountains which were already protecting the *yajna* from the north and south. So the south-west and north-east, two of the intermediate directional points, were chosen. However, the four chosen directions came to include all the castes in the worship of Brahma, adding to Pushkar's appeal by increasing the number of devotees. These four *shivalinga* temples, now form part of the different *parikramas*.

ABOVE *It is often believed that the trideva (Brahma, Vishnu, Shiva) is inseparable and indestructible, but there is no shortage of contrary epigraphical evidence: In 772 CE, Krishnaraja I invoked Shiva and Vishnu in a single verse, omitting Brahma; in the well-known syncretic iconography of Shiva and Vishnu in the composite Harihara form, they are represented with their spouses in the form of Praddyumneshvara in a temple of that name built by Vijayasena of Bengal; Vishnu and Brahma are combined by Virasimha, a Kachhapaghata king near Gwalior, and Shiva and Brahma are worshipped together in the Rewa inscription of Malayasimha. This flexibility is observed, as VS Pathak writes, in the worship of four, eight, or 10* lokapalas *in several* smarta *ceremonies. PV Kane adds in his* History of the Dharmashastra, *that a* dikapati yajna *is performed for the lords of the directions on two occasions: an installation ceremony and when great gifts are given.*

The Three Pushkars

THE THREE PETAL LAKES

The first *parikrama* recommended for pilgrims is around the three Pushkars, created around the three waters formed when three lotus petals dropped from Brahma's hand as he searched for a place for a fire rite. After this consecratory rite, he hoped to stay at Pushkar. But this made access to heaven too easy for humans. Eventually, Brahma decided to live here only on the five days leading to *Kartik Purnima*.

It is said that three fires from the three Pushkars were united for the *yajna* of Brahma. Even today, a *paridhi*, or enclosure, of three green sticks around the altar or three circumambulations of the sacred fire – thrice in a clockwise direction, holding a lighted torch – are supposed to ward off evil spirits. The three Pushkars are naturally associated with the *trimurti*, the Hindu triad represented together in triple form with one body and three heads, or separately as the trinity: Brahma, Vishnu and Shiva. They are also associated with the three Pushkars as patron-deities: Brahma of Jyeshtha or Burha Pushkar, Vishnu of Madhya Pushkar and Shiva of Kanishtha Pushkar.

However, today it seems irrelevant to continue the parallels of the three Pushkars with the three gods of the trinity because Brahma as *rajoguna* – expansiveness and hence activity – would represent passion and desire at the derelict Burha Pushkar; Vishnu's *sattvaguna* – mercy and goodness – would also seem wasted at the abandoned Madhya Pushkar; while Shiva's *tamoguna* – wrath and destruction – would scare the pilgrims, or be attributed to the rewards of Kaliyuga! Popularly, today Brahma is linked to Kanishtha Pushkar.

The crumbled debris of the ancient Aravallis begins to retreat after Nagpahar, and the sands take over. The road straightens between age-old dunes, and a sense of arrival hangs in the air. What seems as a false alarm is actually Jyeshtha or Burha Pushkar, supposedly the old site of the pilgrimage, still dotted with a few temples.

This road to Burha Pushkar was built by the efforts of Shri Krishna Eenani and gets many visitors now. In the drive for modernization to attract the pilgrim-client, a large new marble temple is now under construction here by Swami Janardhanacharya of the Ramanuja sect.

1. JYESHTHA/BURHA/VRIDDHA PUSHKAR 17 21 13

Since Brahma is supposed to have created the lake at Jyeshtha Pushkar, the devotees actually believe that when the rain clouds thunder in the sky, the water level rises at Burha Pushkar. This also makes it sacred to Indra, the lord of rain. The water level here once lay only a metre below the ground and was thus a water source for the neighbourhood. Two notable temples in Burha Pushkar are the Radha-Krishna and Guman Dev Hanuman Temples, the latter with a stepwell where sadhus still live.

There is an interesting legend about how the name 'Burha' Pushkar came about: When Aurangzeb and his army destroyed the temples of Varaha and Keshorai-ji, the Mughal emperor is reported to have asked, "What is the miracle of this place?" He then went to Jyeshtha, the 'senior' Pushkar to wash his face, and a miracle is believed to have taken place – Aurangzeb's hair turned white and his back bent over, converting him into an old man. This Pushkar has since been called 'Burha' Pushkar, or the 'old' Pushkar, from the one which made Aurangzeb old!

BELOW *Shri Ram Ghat of Jyeshtha or Burha Pushkar normally lies dry except in the monsoon. Water from this, once fed Ajmer when Foy Sagar ran dry. Even now, the groundwater level is very high and is supplied to the Western Railway by a mechanized ropeway system.*

2. MADHYA PUSHKAR 15 23 14

Further down the road to Pushkar, on a short, dusty detour to the right, is Madhya Pushkar. Legend has it that the waters dried up at both Jyeshtha and Madhya Pushkar, while the lake at Kanishtha Pushkar, also formed by the dropping of Brahma's lotus petals, finally lured the pilgrims to its shores.

The abandoned Burha Pushkar now has a proper road, but to its west, Madhya Pushkar still lies dry and dormant on a hidden dust track. The *vapi/kund/baye*, or reservoir, of Madhya Pushkar is formed as a large square with the graphic geometry of a series of descending steps, interspersed with steep left-right steps. They create illusions of perspective, especially when shadows from the sun create more steps within steps ingeniously conceived to reach the descending level of water even in the summer season. Despite a recent effort to dig a well, it lies completely dry. A modest temple dedicated to Shiva and a neglected serai for pilgrims was built in 1881 by Pushpartha, a devotee. These are now looked after by the agricultural Rawat community.

All the lakes would have been dry today, were it not for the efforts of the government of Rajasthan in pumping out a continuous flow of water, to "save all the creatures who live in the water" explains a holy man. "The humans come after the other species.... Because man is much more capable of looking after himself, it becomes his duty to protect the others."

BELOW *The grand stepped Prachi Kund of Madhya Pushkar in Nehlia village.*

3. KANISHTHA PUSHKAR

The magnetism of Kanishtha Pushkar – the Pushkar of today – as a site of natural beauty and a Hindu pilgrimage is explained by the Puranas as a place of *padmak yog* where, because of the conjunction of the sun, moon and other satellites, it receives special rays. Amar Nath Pathak of Pushkar says that from March to November, even on breezeless days, the motifs of the earth's magnetic currents can be seen at play on Brahma's waters. This, he believes, has much to do with the specific gravity as the atmospheric pressure combines with its astral planes to produce very special vibrations.

Lalit Panwar, an officer in the Rajasthan government, points to Pushkar's biodiversity which combines different ecosystems with hills, forests, a desert, a lake and rivulets. Here lotuses bloomed till the 19th century (see left and below) – and where now roses blossom in the countryside. It was called Khajurivana, or the forest of date palms. To this Janardhan Sharma adds the list of what is cultivated at Pushkar: millet, sugar cane, rice, date palms and roses, a self-explanatory wonder of mingling products of dry and humid climates with those of tropical and temperate zones.

The elderly Pandit Lal Maharaj-ji complains that once Pushkar Raj had a circumference of 400 *kos* (1,668 kms), now it measures only 20 *kos* (83.40 kms).

Situated at a height of 482 metres above the sea level, Puskar's air currents are well suited for living there throughout the year. The fact that its lake has no outlet but keeps its waters clean through its self-cycling currents, remains a matter of some wonder.

Fig. 17. — Lac de Pochkar, près d'Ajmir (Rajpoutana).

BOTTOM *A late 19th-century photograph of the lotus-filled lake of Pushkar by Raja Deen Dayal.*

FACING PAGE TOP *In* Les Civilisations de l'Inde *by Dr Gustave le Bon, published in 1887, an etching captioned* "Lac de Pochkar, près d'Ajmir (Rajpoutana)"*, shows lotuses abloom on the waters. Commissioned during a 'mission archéologique dans l'Inde', it shows the Zenana Ghat in the foreground where women could bathe within the privacy of a closed room. This is now overbuilt by a temple. In the background are the Chauri Paidi, Karni and Tarni ghats which lie to the west of the lake.*

ABOVE *A langur waits to grab his share of bananas from the pilgrims. The spectacular view of Pushkar from Jamadagni Kund is worth climbing up the steep steps which are painted in blue plastic emulsion and shine in the sun like slabs of ice.*

FOLLOWING PAGES *A sadhu at Saptarishi Ghat.*

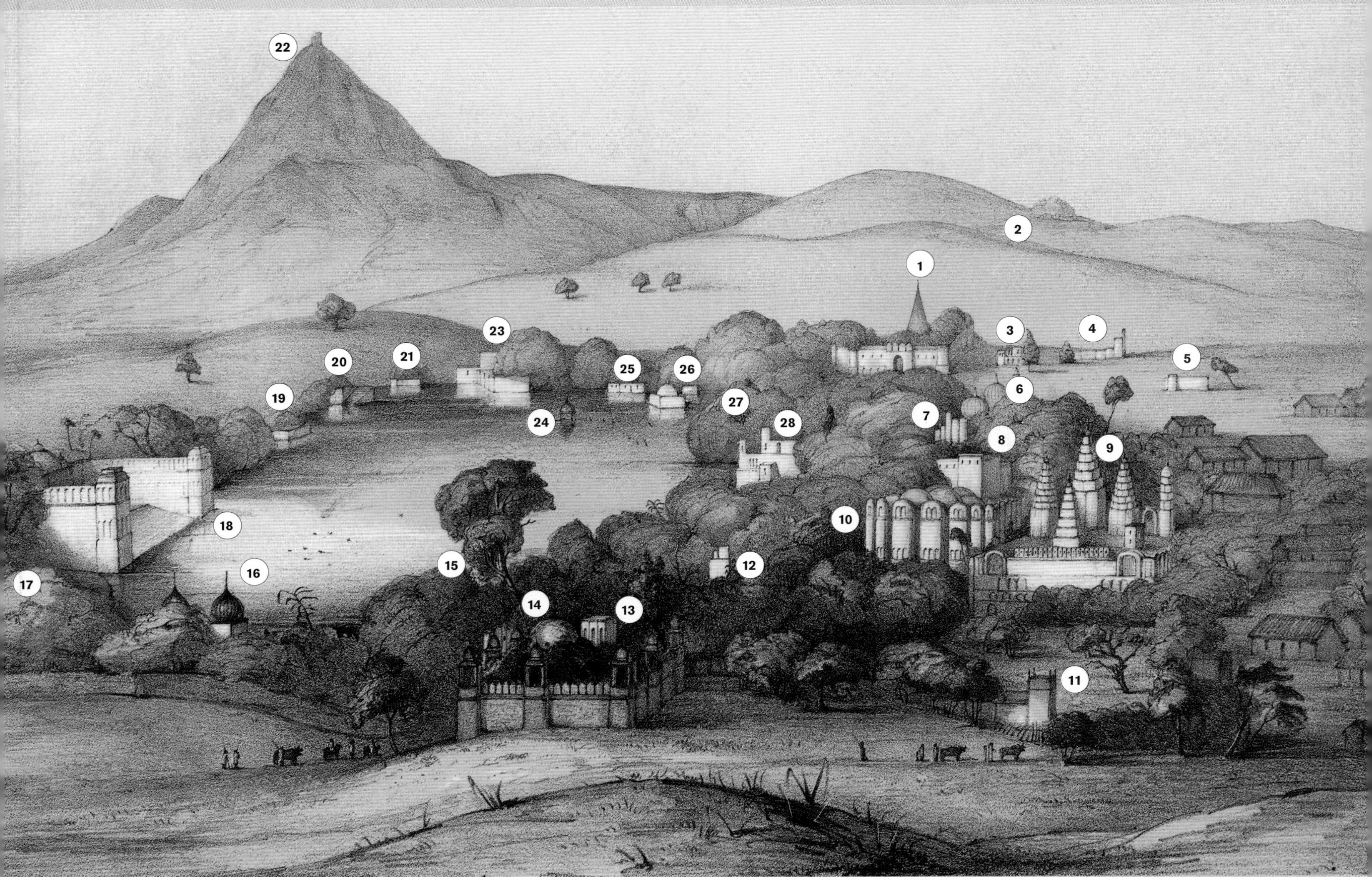

INDEX TO THE ILLUSTRATION

ABOVE *This picturesque and precise landscape of Pushkar is from a folio,* Sketches of Native Life in India..., *by Charles Richard Francis. The Ranganath Venugopal Temple (No 9) seen mid-right with four* shikhar *(spires) and the profile of its gopuram (entrance), was only four years old when this was drawn.*

1. Brahma Temple
2. Kapaleshvar Mahadev Temple
3. Chaturbhuj Badnor Temple
4. Daroga Temple
5. Raj Babra Temple
6. Shahi Masjid
7. Badri Narayan Temple
8. Bhura Narsingh-ji Temple
9. Ranganath Venugopal Temple
10. Ram-Lakshman Temple
11. Bhat Baye/Ganesh Kund
12. Atmateshvar Mahadev Temple
13. Panch Vir Chhatri/Pachdevri
14. Varaha Temple
15. 108 Mahadev Temple
16. Koteshvar Mahadev Temple
17. Man Mandir
18. Mandor-Jodhpur Ghat
19. Swaroop Ghat
20. Kotah Ghat
21. Hingor Mal ka Mahal
22. Savitri Temple
23. Kalyan-ji Temple (Chauri Paidi)
24. Khimsar Chhatri
25. Tarni Ghat
26. Karni Temple
27. Brahma/Yajna Ghat
28. Gau Ghat

LEFT *The Ranganath Venugopal Temple is a mixture of* gopurams *and* shikhars *from the south Indian style, merged with foliated arches and* jharokhas *with pointed eaves. Rousselet was certainly intrigued though he got its description wrong. "It is a curious mixture of every style of architecture, being surmounted by towers, placed close together like the stamba of the Jains, and by the minaret, which is the plan adopted in the Deccan. The outside walls are in the Sikh style; the architecture of the lateral buildings is in the Rajkot style."*

BELOW *Anantprasad Ganeriwal prays before his* pitra guru *Prativadi Bhayankar Ananta Char-ji Maharshi, through whose prayer and ritual he was born to his mother. This* putreshti yajna, *the fire rite for obtaining a son, lasts for 10 days. His meals are still prepared, according to elaborate traditions of privacy, which emphasize hygiene, but can be eaten together with members of all communities. The shaven moustache is also a custom of the Ramanujis.*

BELOW *Although not in any* parikrama *list, the imposing Rama Baikunth Temple is frequently visited because of its location at the entrance of Pushkar. Built in 1924 by two brothers Seth Munginiram-ji and Seth Ram Coowar-ji Bangad of Didwana, this gigantic Vaishnava temple was the second of the Ramanuja sect in Pushkar. Legend has it that the Seth's wife wished to pray at a temple where the doors had shut because she had arrived a minute too late. "If you like praying so much, why don't you make a temple of your own?" the priest rebuked her. Then Vishnu appeared in a dream, asking her husband to go east to Kolkata to seek his fortune. That is when a fortune was made, enabling the making of a second temple of the Ramanuja sect at Pushkar.*

The Ramanujis are easily identified by their sectarian marking on the forehead called vadgal, *or the white, 'U'-shaped mark with a red vertical* tilak *between as a mark of Lakshmi. The 'Y'-shaped or* tengal *mark is also worn within the same sect at the Old Rang-ji Temple. In 1910, when a quarrel over these markings reached the Privy Council in London, a wise compromise was struck. It was ordained that at Vishnu Kanchi, the 'Y'- and 'U'-shaped* tilaks *would be worn for six months each!*

BELOW *The golden* dhvaja sthamba *(flagstaff) surmounted by Garuda, Vishnu's* vahana *(vehicle), at the entrance court of the New Ranganath Temple. It comes from an interesting tradition: such a flagstaff is first mentioned in the Bhilsa inscription of the 2nd century BCE stating that it was erected by Heliodorus, a Greek convert to Vaishnavism.*

THE PUNDITS OF PUSHKAR

PARASHARAS: THE ORIGINAL PUSHKAR PRIESTS Like most legends of upward social mobility and acceptability which are based on the grounds of ability rather than lineage, the Parashara lineage is, by all standards, a convoluted genealogy.

ABOVE *Idols of Parashara, Vyas, Sukhadeva and Peevri Mata in a temple on the main street of Pushkar's Sadar Bazar which comes on the route of the short 5* kos *circumambulation.*

To conceal the real pedigree of the sage Vasishtha, he was said to be born of Brahma but was obliged to leave his body (as retribution for a curse he had given) to be reborn again. This time his parentage was made even more improbable and obscure by giving him two fathers and a mother by suggestion. The two male gods, Mitra and Varuna, emitted their seeds in a pot when they were aroused by the sight of the beautiful nymph Urvashi – a tale which is also repeated with Brahma. The sage Agastya, who has a cave at Pushkar (see p. 189), was also born from this pot. Vasishtha Muni had several wives: Urja, the sister of Sati (Shiva's first wife), who bore him seven sons; a low-born Chandali who gave him his eldest son Shakti or Shaktvi; and Arundhati, considered the faultless and most devoted wife among those of the seven sages.

Shakti continued his father's tradition and married Adrishyanti, a low-caste woman. To carry this low-born genealogy through a caste-cleansing or elevating tale, Shakti was swallowed by a demon for 12 years. During this time his wife kept the baby under her heart. The child began studying the Vedas, reciting them aloud in the womb, benefiting all those who could hear him. This was Parashara, the child prodigy of the scriptures, who studied the Vishnu Purana under Kapila Muni and the Panchatantra under Pulastya Rishi. The former is associated with the ancient pilgrimage of Pushkar and an ashram exits in his name (see p. 187). The sage Parashara was stuck by the beauty of the dark Satyavati, born from a fish, who swallowed her father's seed which was being sent to his mother through a falcon! But Satyavati's body carried an odour of fish, which Parashara promised to remove if she would let him father a famous son. In this tale, Parashara is credited with inventing fog, so that he could make love unseen at midday, midstream, in a boat.

Parashara fathered the renowned sage Vyasa, who is supposed to have written the Mahabharata, and who became the forefather of the Parashara Brahmans – the *tirtha purohits* of Pushkar. They form the majority of Pushkar's Brahmans, and live in Badi Basti – the large settlement.

Legend has it that the Parasharas advised the proud maharaja, Jai Singh II, founder of Jaipur city, not to hold an *ashvamedha yajna* (horse sacrifice) since, as a vassal of the Mughals, he was not a *chakravartin*, or universal ruler. But with the decline of the later Mughals and the power vacuum in Delhi, Jai Singh wanted to assert his strength and saw himself playing a larger role in its politics. Establishing or extending territorial boundaries was one of the traditional functions of a horse sacrifice. According to the ritual, the dead horse was put in a pit covered with a sheet, and the *rani*, or queen, was supposed to make the motion of a sexual union. The revival of this Aryan fertility rite, however symbolic, in the mid-18th century, supposedly amused the Rani of Jaipur, who burst out laughing. This was interpreted as a sin by the Brahman-dominated society and the royal family had to visit Pushkar to atone for this sin.

GAUDAS: THE LATE ARRIVALS Raja Jai Singh arrived at Pushkar and wanted to offer *prayashchita daan* – a retributional charity – after his prayers. But as it happened it was a day of the solar eclipse – considered inauspicious for receiving gifts – so the Parashara Brahmans refused. Taking this refusal as a royal affront, the raja immediately replaced the priest with his own – a Gauda Brahman. The arrival of the Gauda Brahmans at Pushkar thus dates back only to the 18th century.

The Gauda Brahmans, originally of Bengal where they are called Sanadhya, supposedly came to Delhi and Jaipur with the armies of Raja Man Singh of Amber when he went to the east as commander of the Mughal forces of Akbar. Subsequently, more Gauda Brahmans settled here to counter the monopoly and malevolence of the Parashara Brahmans. The Gaudas stay in Jaisinghpura, now called Chhoti Basti, or small settlement, and have maintained a tense and contentious relationship with the Parasharas of Badi Basti, or big settlement. The Gauda Brahmans believe that the Parasharas are Shakadvipis – foreigners who hail from Persia, as their name suggests.

Similar to the Pushkar Brahmans, the Audicha or Avadich Brahmans of Idar, Gujarat, worship the Brahma Temple in Khedbrahma and call themselves Kheda Brahmans.

The Parasharas, although priests, were given large *jagirs*, and began to behave like landed Rajput chieftains – which also included looting others! The Parasharas justified this by saying that they had learnt this from the Rajput rajas. Jai Singh of Jaipur retaliated and wrote to all the princes not to patronize the Parasharas who had become thieves and looters. As a result, the ruling houses of Bikaner, Kashmir, Alwar and Neemrana stopped using their services. The Parasharas retaliated against the Gauda Brahmans by excluding the temples and ghats under the charge of the Gaudas from the official lists of the *parikramas*.

Louis Rousselet, travelled to Pushkar from 11 to 16th April, in 1878. His account also elaborates the tensions between the rulers and the priests:

> *This lake soon became a favourite resort of pilgrims, and during the Middle Ages the princely families of India vied with one another in covering its banks with temples and cenotaphs. Gradually quite a town of religious buildings sprang up, peopled by Brahmins. The wealthy pilgrims from all parts of India brought untold riches to Poshkur, and the princes spared no expense to enrich the holy inhabitants of the sacred town. Tod gives us an anecdote which the Brahmins never fail to relate to visitors, showing to what a pitch the folly of the Hindoo princes was carried in the ostentatious charity. The kings of Jeypore and Joudpore, always rivals in war, love, or folly, were in the habit of making an annual pilgrimage to Poshkur. On their arrival, they each ordered some scales to be filled with precious things, such as jewels, gold, and costly materials, which were piled up until the amount equalled their own weight; and the whole was then distributed among the Brahmins. The King of Jeypore had the advantage of possessing a well-filled treasure and a rich country, while his rival, on the other hand, being chief of a race of warriors and of vast domains, received but a scanty revenue from lands barely reclaimed from the desert; but at Poshkur riches carried the day against valour. One day, when the two princes were in the scales, the Rajah of Jeypore made a cutting remark on the poverty of the offerings of his relation and rival; and by the advice of his minister, a very intelligent man, the Rahtore Rajah defied the other ever to make as great a concession to the Brahmins as he would. The challenge was accepted : upon which the Rahtore exclaimed, "All the lands in my kingdom, occupied at this moment by Brahmins, shall be sahsun from henceforth and for ever!" His rival of Jeypore was about to outdo him, when his minster, throwing himself before him, prevented him from uttering the words which would irreparably have ruined his kingdom.*

ABOVE *Kalyan Mal Shastri, a prominent Parashara Brahman of Pushkar (top), and Hathi Ram Mishra (bottom), a leading member of the Gauda Brahmans.*

FACING PAGE *Walking on the streets of Pushkar is literally like participating in a live carnival. Every minute holds an unpredictable surprise.*

BELOW *A fakir flaunts his many rings. Many fakirs who visit the* dargah *at Ajmer also wander over to Pushkar. Some of them set up pavement shops to sell semi-precious stones connected to birth signs and horoscopes.*

FAKIRS

About the origins of the Naga ascetics the informants gave the following depiction: From ancient times the Naga ascetics were peregrinating in the country in groups, called Jhundi. During the reign of Akbar, the Moslem Malanga faquirs were troubling the Hindu villagers, because the Hindus used to receive the Naga sanyasis respectfully while the Malanga faquirs were more feared than respected. This eventually exploded into an open clash between the Nagas and the Malangas. The Malangas were already equipped with swords, they killed the Naga ascetics mercilessly. When the Hindus approached Akbar for justice, the latter said: two cows are fighting, which indicated his helplessness or non-interference in this religious matter. On this the princes of Rajputana sent some soldiers in the guise of ascetics to defend the Hindu sanyasis and villagers from the ravages of the Malanga faquirs. It was on this occasion that for the first time the Naga ascetics were supplied with arms by Hindu kings. These ascetics gradually trained themselves in fighting, and subsequently fought many battles and took part in many a skirmish. In the case of the Sikhs, the arms were given to them only by the 9th Guru, but the Sikh as a sect existed from the time of Guru Nanak. Similarly the Naga sannyasis were organized much before the arms were supplied to them by the Hindu princes during the Moslem rule in India.

— SURAJIT SINHA & SARASWATI BAIDYANATH
Ascetics of Kashi

BEHRUPIA

An elder *behrupia*, or one who disguises himself as different people, uses this

transformation ingeniously to make a living. One day he may become a god, another simply a policeman. His skills lie in changing his word and lines according to his fancy dress. A *behrupia* dressed in a tinsel veil and jingle bells was reciting a poem, *"Main Mewar ki Rani hoon* (I am the queen of Udaipur)."

"Such human curiosa were (and are) aspects of India that fascinate foreigners. We gaze at them a bit sheepishly and uncomprehendingly, bewildered by all the levels they represent: the superficial one of plumes and weird gadgets; the worldly one of a hand reaching for a rupee; and another that keeps alive an age of faith." writes Stuart Cary Welch describing a miniature of the same subject.

SADHUS

Whereas the Brahmans form the hereditary priestly class, which have carried forward the teachings of Hinduism, the sadhus can be from any caste. These are usually men and women (*sadhavis*) who have lived their worldly life and now seek what the material world can no longer provide. As wandering, holy mendicants, their hardships and austerities, born from their denial of worldly pleasures builds *tapas*, or heat, believed to give them powers to bless the lowly mortals absorbed in worldly pursuits. Pushkar is a natural home for these rootless sadhus who wander from one holy pilgrimage to another while also migrating to the Himalayas during summer.

ABOVE *"The sketch represents three Hindu women in their morning expedition to the Lake," wrote CR Francis in 1848, who also sketched them. "Alligators abound and are not allowed to be molested. On the other side of the lake, opposite to the principal mass of buildings, these creatures may be seen with their snouts and upper part of their bodies out of the water. The author has seen them, whilst taking his evening ride, enjoying the air in great numbers."*

In 1878, an optimistic appraisal of the Pushkar crocodiles was recorded in the diary of Louis Rousselet: "Even before the sun appears above the far distant peaks on the horizon, inhabitants and pilgrims all hasten to wash in the healing waters. A thousand bathers appear and disappear among the limpid waves, defying the alligators, who, frightened by the noise, keep at a distance."

CROCODILE MYTHS & RECORDS

NOVEMBER 1928: *In Pushkar there is a holy lake surrounded on three sides by several bathing ghats, temples and privately owned abodes with janana bathing ghats protected by thick lime and concrete jalis to ward off the attacks of man-eating crocodiles.*

The yearly holy mela was in full swing and millions had collected from all over the country to have a holy dip in the sacred tank. On the 6th of November, at about 11 am, a great deal of shouting started on the bathing ghats and we all rushed to the verandah of the Bharatpur Kunj where I was staying. Overlooking the lake we saw a man swimming in the lake. In spite of warnings from the crowd on the bathing ghats to return immediately to the ghats because of the danger of the crocodiles, the man ignored them all as he was determined to commit suicide, and kept going further and further in the tank. This desperado had a small stick (dunda) of about two feet in his hand.

Within five minutes a crocodile saw the man and started moving towards him. This increased the hue and cry from the crowds to an ear splitting volume, by which time the desperado too had seen the fast-approaching crocodile and prepared himself to fight it out. In the meanwhile two or three crocodiles too had seen the man and were swimming fast towards him. As the first crocodile made the final rush, the brave man gave the crocodile a strong blow with his stick on its snout and we were amazed to see the crocodile give up the idea of catching the man and made a retreat. In the meanwhile the other crocodiles approached the man to receive the same treatment. Once two of them rushed towards the man, who wisely kept a sharp look out and just as they closed in on him simultaneously from two opposite directions, he managed to dive under water and the two rushing crocodiles collided with one another. By this time a monster crocodile of about 16 feet in length, sitting and basking itself on a pukka chhatri in the middle of the lake, seeing all this hubbub going on from about fifty yards away, had slid down the chhatri and swam rapidly towards the scene. When about fifteen yards away from the man, this ugly monster dived under water and within a couple of seconds the unfortunate, brave man simply vanished. The monster had carried him away. The entire crowd on the bathing ghats were dazed with sorrow. Then the identity of the man was disclosed: a Jat youth from a close-by village in Nagaur District in Marwar. That he had two wives who quarreled daily making his life miserable. Fed up with his beauty queens, the poor Jat had decided to commit suicide in a unique manner. At about 4 pm there was another uproar from the crowd on the bathing ghats and we again rushed to the verandah to see a troop of about twelve crocodiles chasing the large monster which was swimming fast ahead of them with the poor dead man's body trunk in its mouth. Both the legs, the head, and both the hands of the man had been severed and snatched away from its trunk by the other crocos but the monster was not prepared to part away with the trunk and wanted to keep it as its own share. The crowds at the ghats were making a hell of the din and row. The monster, after having made two rounds of the entire lake, suddenly threw itself up above the water, then resting on its enormous tail, jerked the dead man's trunk in the air and swallowed it as it was falling back. When the monster fell back with a huge splash on the water, everything was over. There was now nothing left for the other crocodiles to share and they all dispersed in different directions, and there was a pin drop silence on the ghats for a minute or two.

— RAO SAHIB SHRI KESHAV SEN OF KHARWA, *Unpublished Diary*

The Rao Sahib grew up to represent India at the Rome Olympics, 1964. The incident was keenly observed and recalled by him, even though he was only seven years old when it occured

ABOVE *The thought of being eaten by a crocodile while on a pilgrimage can hardly be comforting. But mythological tales (as depicted above) such as that of Gajendramoksha – when Mahavishnu tests the Pandyan king, Indradyumna who had turned into an elephant for 1,000 years, before killing the crocodile – provide solace for simple pilgrims. Arjuna, one of the five Pandavas, who spent the last year of his exile incognito at Pushkar was also connected to a crocodile tale in the waters of Puri. Blessed by Ulupi's boon, Arjuna stepped into the water to rid it of crocodiles at the sage's request. When he dragged out a large crocodile who had caught his leg, it turned into a celestial nymph, once cursed by a sage.*

APRIL 1933: *The lake is full of crocodiles, which are worshipped and fed by pious hands, but this does not prevent the creatures from carrying off any unwary dog or calf which may stray into the water. Sometimes a human being falls a prey, and a strange incident which occurred some days ago illustrates with gruesome vividness the boldness and tenacity of the reptiles. A traveller had brought his pony down to drink and was standing by it in the water when a crocodile approached unawares and seized his leg. The man had the presence of mind to throw his arms round the pony's neck; the frightened animal rushed away from the brink, dragging with it the man and the crocodile with its jaws still firmly gripping the leg of the victim. His cries brought out a crowd of the inhabitants, who belaboured the beast with sticks, but totally without effect, for as soon as the man's hold of the pony relaxed, the brute resolutely carried him back across the sand to the lake and disappeared with him for ever into its depths, in spite of the frantic but unavailing efforts of the mob to arrest its progress.*

— CW WADDINGTON, CIE, MVO,
Indian India: As Seen by a Guest in Rajastahan

Principal of the Rajkumar College, Rajkot, Kathiawar and the Mayo College, Ajmer, Rajputana

The crocodiles of Pushkar were finally removed to the Chambal river valley in 1955. This delay may well have been because the crocodile continued to be worshipped as much as to be feared. It is considered holy since it is the mount of the river goddess Ganga.

RIGHT *The carcasses of a crocodile and its baby, untreated by a taxidermist, lie by the Narsingh Ghat, reminding pilgrims of the dangers which were once present for the bathers.*

The Three Parikramas

Legend has it that after Brahma's *yajna* was over, he asked all the Brahmans to circumambulate the holy lake. This is believed to be the origin of the sacred *parikrama,* the circumambulating tradition for pilgrims. Just as there are three Pushkars, there are also three *parikramas* of varying lengths demanding different degrees of perseverance.

ABOVE *Leather is considered impure by the pandits who are the keepers of the temples and the ghats. To save insult to their gods and embarrassment to those alien to the Hindu traditions, several boards of caution have been painted, often with an innocence which is as amusing as it is touching, as in: "Put of your shoes hear!"*

PARIKRAMA NOTES & ALBUM
For a detailed account and explanation of the pilgrimage, see pp. 182–195.

THE GROUNDING

There is no rigidity in the order or sequence prescribed for the pilgrimage at Pushkar. The geographical location of the *dharamshala* or hotel where one may stay, and other factors such as the need for the veneration of a particular deity, the time available and the mode of transport decide the order and extent of a pilgrim's journey. However, two principles must be followed: all pilgrims are required to circumambulate the lake in a clockwise direction, and they have to visit the temple of Brahma, their *raison d'etre* of being in Pushkar.

Before beginning any *parikrama* it is first advised to take permission from the priest, bathe in the holy waters of Sarovar, the lake of Pushkar, and then proceed with the *pandit.* The pilgrim is addressed as *yajamaan*, or sacrificer, and the priest is regarded as a medium in helping the pilgrim perform the ritual. However, in reality, the long history of pilgrim harassment by the Brahmans has ironically reversed the role – much like Brahma in the Pushkar legend – it is the sacrificer who becomes the sacrifice during the elaborate rituals. Louis Rousselet strikes a similar note, way back in 1878 when he spent four days at Pushkar. "The newly arrived pilgrim repairs forthwith to the *ghats* for the ceremony of initiation, when fierce contention for possession of the client arises among the Brahmin's; each one of whom seizes the unfortunate traveller by some part of his clothing, offering him a thousand advantages, and promising to perform the ceremony better and cheaper than his rival."

BELOW *Simple pilgrims are easily exploited for donations in the name of their ancestors.*

But Rousselet records the contrast whereby "if some rich individual came to wash away his sins in the sacred waters, he is at once surrounded by the Brahmin's, who load him with flattery, and are as humble and cringing to him as they are haughty and insolent to the poorer pilgrims. Even the kings of Rajasthan have become cold and sceptical, and think more of filling their treasuries than despoiling themselves of the benefit of the Brahmins."

THE PILGRIMAGE SITES

The chronological order suggested in the lists for each of the three *parikramas* ensures that all the sites are included, even though it entails one shorter circle which spirals out clockwise and meets a larger one to include the peripheral pilgrim spots in a centripetal whirl.

SHUDDHA VAPI/GAYA KUND 16 20 15

Between Burha and Madhya Pushkar lies Shuddha Vapi whose reservoir is also called Gaya Kund with an amazing stepwell. Today, after visiting Burha or Jyeshtha Pushkar, only a decreasing numbers of deeply superstitious pilgrims or those with family members who suffer from psychological problems, go to ward off evil spirits at Shuddha Vapi, or Gaya Kund, the purifying reservoir.

The Padma Purana mentions that Rama came here for the *shradh* of his father King Dasharatha, since the waters of this tank supposedly drive away ghosts and evil spirits and bring moksha. A *pinda-daan* to the Brahmans is particularly stressed. On *Shukl Paksha Chaturthi Mangalvar* they believe that the Ganga brings its waters to this tank.

THE 7.5 KOS PARIKRAMA (two days) *The pilgrim begins the first day with the following temples located around the lake:*

1. Varaha Temple
2. Neelkanth Mahadev Temple
3. Atmateshvar Mahadev Temple
4. Gupteshvar Mahadev Temple
5. Bhuteshvar Mahadev Temple
6. Bihari-ji/Bai-ji Temple
7. Uttaramukhi Balaji
8. Chaturnath/Bavan Bhairon Temple
9. Brahma Temple

Leaving the immediate locale of the lake, the pilgrim proceeds to the subsequent sites:

10. Kapaleshvar Mahadev Temple
11. Kalika Mata Temple
12. Papmochini Temple
13. Hanuman Baori
14. Bhat Baye/Ganesh Kund
15. Madhya Pushkar
16. Shuddha Vapi/Gaya Kund
17. Jyeshtha/Burha Pushkar

Jyeshtha Pushkar marks the end of the first day's journey, and halt for the night. The second day begins at Leela Sevri village, and takes the pilgrim to the following locations:

18. Lal Bihari Radha Madhav Temple
19. Kapileshvar Mahadev/Kapil Muni Ashram
20. Pandeshvar Mahadev Temple
21. Gau Mukh
22. Panch Kund
23. Jamadagni Kund
24. Devrani-Jethani Baori
25. Pushkarni/Shivanand Ashram
26. Vamadev Gufa
27. Vishvamitra Ashram/Gadh Baye-Narol
28. Agastya Muni Gufa
29. Shri Ram Jharokha
30. Puruhuta Shakti Peeth/Chamunda Mata Temple

At this point, the pilgrim is advised to return from the outskirts to Chaturnath Bhairon Temple, and proceed to:

31. Mahaprabhu-ji ki Baithak
32. Parashuram Dwar
33. Brahma Ghat
34. Yajna Ghat
35. Badri Narayan Temple
36. Ranganath Venugopal/Old Rang-ji Temple
37. Gau Ghat
38. Ram-Lakshman Temple

This marks the end of the parikrama, *with the pilgrim returning to Varaha Ghat.*

THE 24 KOS PARIKRAMA (three to four days) *The following sequence takes the pilgrim through this middle-range circumambulation:*

Start at Leela Sevri village

1. Lal Bihari Radha Madhav Temple
2. Pandeshvar Mahadev Temple
3. Gau Mukh
4. Panch Kund
5. Jamadagni Kund
6. Vamadev Gufa
7. Vishvamitra Ashram/Gadh Baye-Narol (*first night*)
8. Adhar Shila
9. Agastya Muni Gufa
10. Puruhuta Shakti Peeth/Chamunda Mata Temple
11. Sankatamochan Barh Ganesh Temple
12. Savitri Temple
13. Nanda-Prachi-Sarasvati Sangam
14. Nandrai Mata
15. Kakreshvar-Makreshvar Temples
16. Kanbaye (*second night*)
17. Kalika Mata Temple
18. Papmochini Temple
19. Hanuman Baori
20. Shuddha Vapi/Gaya Kund
21. Jyeshtha/Burha Pushkar (*third night*)
22. Badar Mata
23. Madhya Pushkar
24. Vaidyanath Mahadev Temple
25. Makrol Mata/Markandey Ashram
26. Lomash Rishi/Rojari Mata

THE 84 KOS PARIKRAMA (four to seven days) *This extended* parikrama *includes the peripheral pilgrimages. The major stop-overs are:*

1. Kanbaye
2. Kakreshvar-Makreshvar Temples
3. Nanda-Prachi-Sarasvati Sangam
4. Nandrai Mata
5. Shiva Temple, Thanvla
6. Bhairav Nath, Thanvla
7. Bada Asan
8. Baval Mata
9. Vaidyanath Mahadev Temple
10. Makrol Mata/Markandey Ashram
11. Lomash Rishi/Rojari Mata
12. Badar Mata
13. Jyeshtha/Burha Pushkar
14. Madhya Pushkar
15. Shuddha Vapi/Gaya Kund
16. Bhat Baye/Ganesh Kund
17. Ardhachandrashekhar Mahadev Temple, Ajmer
18. Nimbarkacharya, Salemabad
19. Ated Mata, Ajmer
20. Kalpavriksha, Sardhana
21. Gauri Kund, Sardhana
22. Lal Bihari Radha Madhav Temple
23. Ghati ke Hanuman Temple
24. Bhanvta Devi Temple
25. Kudki
26. Ajaypal
27. Pushkar Raj
28. Kanbaye

ABOVE *A simple fire ceremony of the Bhuta-Preta puja rids pilgrims of evil spirits before they begin their pilgrimage of Pushkar.*

TOP *Shuddha Vapi is a gigantic, square stepwell between Burha and Madhya Pushkar where bathers leave old clothes behind in an act of purification. Since Shuddha Vapi may not be accessible to all ages, often effigies or carved representations of those infested with evil spirits are left by the Gaya Kund to ward off the evil eye.*

A handbook by Lal Chandra Sharma Gaur offers a longer list which begins and ends at Pushkar. The distance and time necessary for this is not easy to calculate: Pushkar, Kanbaye, Nanda-Prachi-Sarasvati, Nand, Govindgarh, Alniyavas, Kudki (Mirabai's birthplace), Thanvla, Tilora, Kodel, Majhevala (Dugarya), Lomash Rishi, Vaidyanath, Markandey Ashram, Makadvali, Banval, Ramdeora, Salemabad, Karkedi, Piplad, Parbatsar, Kinsariya, Rupangarh, Ralavata, Kishangarh, Khoda Ganesh-ji, Pitambar ki Gal, Chhota Udaipur, Chorasiyavas, Dorai, Mangaliyavas, Makreda, Bhanvta, Pichholia, Ajaypal, Bijoliya, Bhagvanpura, Pushkar.

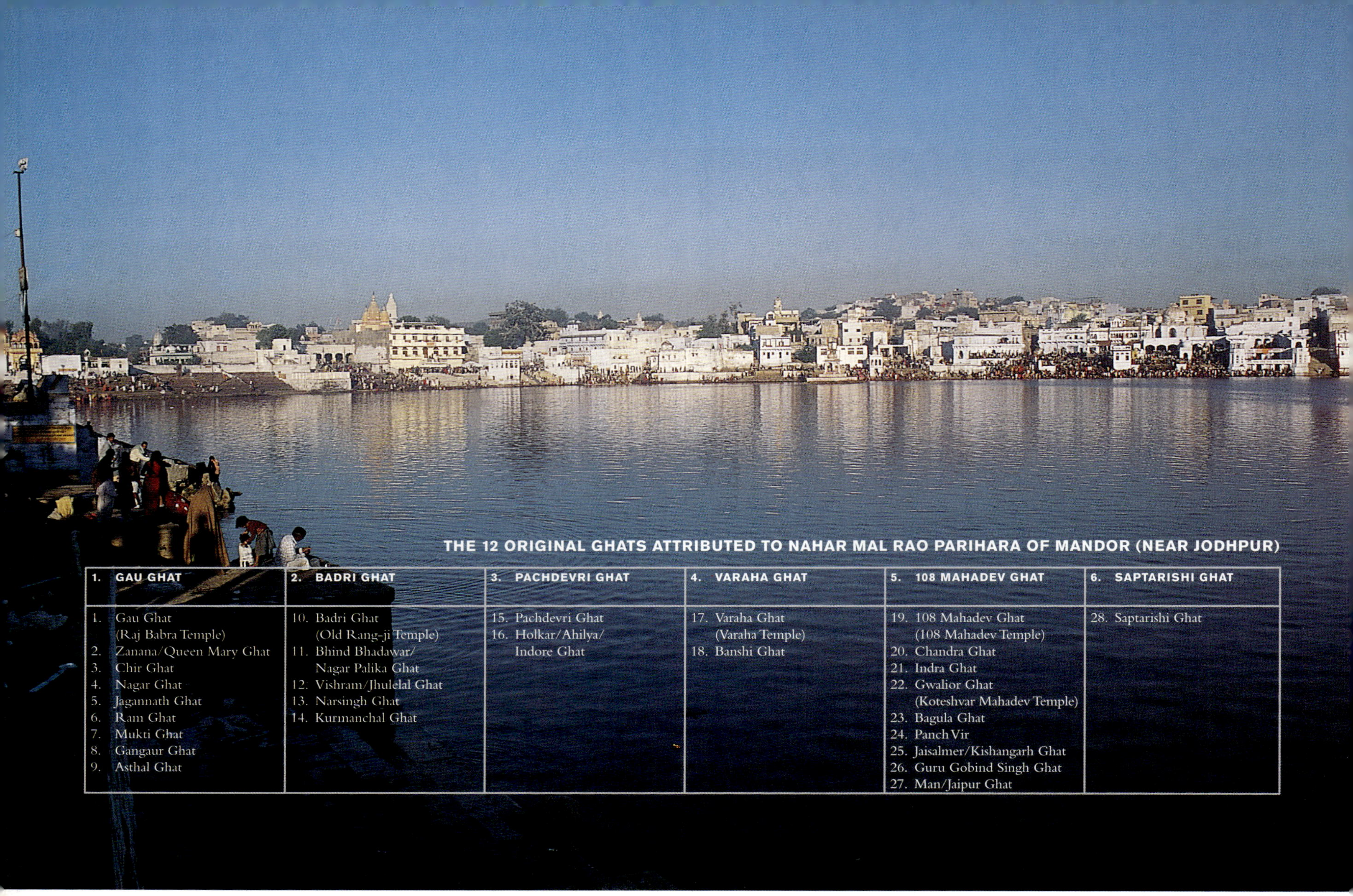

THE 12 ORIGINAL GHATS ATTRIBUTED TO NAHAR MAL RAO PARIHARA OF MANDOR (NEAR JODHPUR)

1. GAU GHAT	2. BADRI GHAT	3. PACHDEVRI GHAT	4. VARAHA GHAT	5. 108 MAHADEV GHAT	6. SAPTARISHI GHAT
1. Gau Ghat (Raj Babra Temple) 2. Zanana/Queen Mary Ghat 3. Chir Ghat 4. Nagar Ghat 5. Jagannath Ghat 6. Ram Ghat 7. Mukti Ghat 8. Gangaur Ghat 9. Asthal Ghat	10. Badri Ghat (Old Rang-ji Temple) 11. Bhind Bhadawar/ Nagar Palika Ghat 12. Vishram/Jhulelal Ghat 13. Narsingh Ghat 14. Kurmanchal Ghat	15. Pachdevri Ghat 16. Holkar/Ahilya/ Indore Ghat	17. Varaha Ghat (Varaha Temple) 18. Banshi Ghat	19. 108 Mahadev Ghat (108 Mahadev Temple) 20. Chandra Ghat 21. Indra Ghat 22. Gwalior Ghat (Koteshvar Mahadev Temple) 23. Bagula Ghat 24. Panch Vir 25. Jaisalmer/Kishangarh Ghat 26. Guru Gobind Singh Ghat 27. Man/Jaipur Ghat	28. Saptarishi Ghat

the sandy mela *grounds, which lead on to the vast desert plains of Marwar.*

PUSHKAR PARIKRAMAS: THE THREE CIRCUMAMBULATI

7.5 KOS 24 KOS 84 KOS PARIKRAMAS

1 KOS: 4.17 KILOMETRES OR 2 MILES

BHANVTA DEVI TEMPLE 24
40 kms W

NANDRAI MATA 14 4
9 kms W

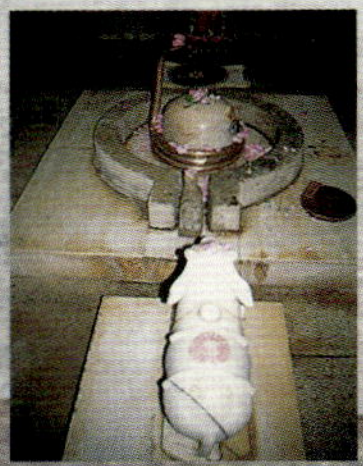

KAKRESHVAR-MAKRESHVAR TEMPLES 15 2
11 kms W

NANDA-PRACHI-SARASVATI SANGAM 13 3
12 kms SW

SAVITRI TEMPLE 12
4 kms SW

KANBAYE 16 1
10 kms SW

AJAYPAL 26
15 kms SW

SANKATAMOCHAN BARH GANESH TEMPLE 11
2 kms SW

PURUHUTA SHAKTI PEETH/ CHAMUNDA MATA TEMPLE 30 10
3 kms SW

Kudki Mahadev and Bhanval Mata in Kudki (45 kms W), the birthplace of Mirabai, also form a part of a long 84 *kos parikrama*. Some devotees even go to Keshorai Patan to see the idol of Krishna which was removed from Pushkar to save its desecration by Aurangzeb when a mosque replaced a temple.

Koteshvar Mahadev, Chandra-Surya Temple, 108 Mahadev and the New Rang-ji Temple are not on the *parikrama* lists of Pushkar because they are managed by the Gauda Brahmans, or south Indian priests, and not the Parasharas who consider themselves the *raj purohits*, or the ruling priests, of the pilgrimage.

DISTANCES & DIRECTIONS ARE APPROXIMATE INDICATIONS ONLY. ALL DISTANCES ARE FROM PUSHKAR.

ONS
SHIVA TEMPLE 5
Thanvla
13 kms NW
BHAIRAV NATH 6
Thanvla
14 kms NW
BADA ASAN 7
16 kms NW
BAVAL MATA 8
30 kms NE
BADRI NARAYAN TEMPLE 35
VAIDYANATH MAHADEV TEMPLE 24
10 kms NE
RAM-LAKSHMAN TEMPLE 38
KAPALESHVAR MAHADEV TEMPLE 10
RANGANATH VENUGOPAL/ OLD RANG-JI TEMPLE 36
BRAHMA TEMPLE 9
GAU GHAT 37
YAJNA GHAT 34
BRAHMA GHAT 33
PARASHURAM DWAR 32
MAHAPRABHU-JI KI BAITHAK 31
CHATURNATH/ BAVAN BHAIRON TEMPLE 8
AGASTYA MUNI GUFA 28 9
5 kms S
SHRI RAM JHAROKHA 29
6 kms S
ADHAR SHILA 8
8 kms uphill S
View from VISHVAMITRA ASHRA
GADH BAYE-NAROL
6 kms uphill S

7TH CENTURY CE & THE 52 GHATS TODAY WITH OLD/NEW TEMPLES BUILT ON OR NEAR THE GHATS

7. MANDOR/GURJARA GHAT	8. SWARUP GHAT	9. HINGOR MAL KA MAHAL	10. KALYAN GHAT	11. BRAHMA GHAT	12. YAJNA GHAT
29. Mandor/Jodhpur/ Gorakhnathi Ghat 30. Bundi Ghat 31. Krishna Ghat 32. Balunda Ghat 33. Vir Gurjara Ghat 34. Sikar Ghat	35. Swarup Vallabh Ghat (Savitri Temple) 36. Kota Ghat	37. Hingor Mal Mahal/ Tantuvaya Vaishya Ghat 38. Chauri Paidi Ghat	39. Kalyan Ghat (Rama Baikunth Temple) 40. Raj Bohra Ghat 41. Karni Ghat 42. Tarni Ghat 43. Parashuram Ghat (Nimbark) 44. Savitri Ghat	45. Brahma Ghat (Brahma Temple) 46. Dadhicha/Hada Ghat 47. Sati Ghat	48. Yajna Ghat (Riddhi-Siddhi Temple) 49. Shitla Mata Ghat 50. Chhik Mata Ghat 51. Bharatpur Ghat 52. Rehgaran/Gandhi/ Shaheed Ghat

View of the Sarovar and the northern ghats of Pushkar from the Gorakhnathi ashram.

Instead of waiting for his wife Savitri to arrive at the yajna, *the impatient Brahma – who required a wife to start it – married Gayatri, the Gurjara girl, in haste. It is nevertheless worth observing that Gayatri was the faultless wife who atoned for her husband's sin at being impatient. For this reason, the Papmochini Temple (also called the Gayatri Peeth) is where retribution for sins is easily granted.*

श्री गोरक्षनाथ मंदिर भेषबारह पंथ दलीचा
फोन नं. 72536

GORAKHNATHIS

The Gorakhnathis have a long lineage chequered with many occult Buddhist, Shaivite and Tantric beliefs as opposed to the Vedantic teachings of Shankaracharya. Originally believed to be named after a Natha yogi, Gorakhnath or Goraksha (keeper or protector of cows), the cult is variously traced back to between the 9th and 12th centuries CE. Gorakhnath is a 'descendant' of Adinath, a *siddha* who attained occult powers through yoga. His adherents are distinguished by long, split ears pierced with looped earrings, giving them the popular name of *kanphata* yogis, or the split-eared ascetics.

The tutelary deity of Nepal, Matsyendranath, was the first incarnate teacher of the Nath sect and in Mahayana Buddhism he is identified with the *bodhisattva* Avalokiteshvara. Gorakhnath is also identified by the Tibetan historian Taranath as his pupil, and it is he who gives the Gorkhas of Nepal their name. Pashupatinath in Nepal is an important centre of the Gorakhnathis.

Above the ancient Jodhpur Ghat, that may well have been the first one built by Nahar Mal Rao Parihar of Mandor in the 7th century CE, the Gorakhnathis have now made an ashram and temple with an elongated, modern *shikhar.* Their magical and alchemical practices, which became very popular after the 12th century, still appeal greatly to lay worshippers. Historically, Gorakhnath is associated with Gorakhpur in western Uttar Pradesh, but because of his occult powers, many magical myths are also related to his birth and existence. Gorakhnath is also credited with authoring a book on Hatha Yoga, now lost. Among the miraculous deeds attributed to him are the withholding of rain, the power to revive the dead and the indefinite prolongation of his own life. Although this belief cuts across the theory of karma where one's actions in this and previous lives decide the length of one's life, the envisaged extension of life was supposedly generated by yogic powers.

ABOVE & ABOVE LEFT *The illuminated temple stands out against the backdrop of the dark hill, and (left) silhouetted against a monsoon sky.*

FACING PAGE *A Gorakhnathi, stands outside the Mahayogi Machhendra Nath Temple of his sect watching stone workers craft capitals for the Baba Mastanath Dvara. In the absence of any norms or restrictions, constant embellishments have unfortunately marred the architectural purity and unity of the ghats and temples of Pushkar which compete in their decorative cement work and now pink ceramic tiles.*

The Gorakhnathi *langar* feeds thousands of pilgrims daily during the Pushkar *mela*.

OASIS IN THE SAND

SANDS OF TIME

Geologists aver that 14 million years ago, the desert of Rajasthan lay beneath the vast Tethys sea. Seashells and fossils have been unearthed from the sands, confirming this theory. Today, ploughs optimistically pattern the sands, hoping for the mercy of the rain gods. The timeless desert has a metaphysical quality, honed by the forced austerity of life within it and the sheer struggle for existence. Even so, the Rajasthani people have learned to celebrate the monotonous palette of the landscape, by adorning it with their multi-hued fabrics and crafts.

According to local myth, the imposing desert was Brahma's creation by the sand he threw to combat an accidental fire caused by an inebriated Shiva. In an eternity of shifting dunes and valleys, time cannot be measured here in terms of hourglasses. The Hindu calendar originated from Brahma and is based on a cyclic concept of life and rebirth (see p. 21).

In 1878, Louis Rousselet recorded, "On the 11th of April we marched towards Poshkur, a sacred oasis situated on the edge of the desert... It is impossible to imagine a more striking contrast than that which existed between this panorama and the country which met our eye view on the other side of the defile. Hills of sand rise on all sides up to the very summit of the Aravallis, and seem as though endeavouring to cross this barrier, which alone prevents them from overrunning the valley of Ajmere; the desert stretches to the horizon; and here and there jagged peaks, blackened as if by fire, break the monotony of its undulating surface."

PAGES 76-77 *Morning mist and smoke clothe Pushkar's landscape in mysticism while the green trees announce the waters beyond.*

FACING PAGE *An aerial view of the furrows that mark the sandy fields, interspersed with the graphic grid of water channels.*

FOLLOWING PAGES *Today, just as sprinklers have reduced the dependence on unreliable rains, tractors have made the farmer's life easier.*

BELOW *A sand beetle imprints the timeless, but fickle sand ripples with its ephemeral footprints.*

RIGHT & BELOW *Pushkar was once a haven for the white lotus, the seat of Brahma. The greed of the lotus vendors as well as recurring droughts have ensured that no lotus can now be found here. But floriculture still flourishes. Ganesh Ram does the rounds of the blooming fields, selects, negotiates and carries fragrant bundles tied in cloth. Flowers are cut only around sunrise and sunset, sprayed with water and then sold.*

ABOVE & RIGHT *The darter is distinguished by its sinuous neck, which gives it the common name of the snake bird. Living by the waters, it is the most specialized water-fisher. Its neck bones dart forward like a trigger when it spears its prey by a quick straightening of its neck. Darters breed in swampy lowlands and fly with their fanned-out tails.*

FAR RIGHT *The Indian eagle-owl is recognized even at night by its deep, sonorous double hoot. It is not scared to show itself by day, but other birds often mob it, aware of its poor daylight visibility. It is an impressive, alert-looking bird at home in rocky country with light, scrubby woodlands.*

RIGHT *A common hoopoe and a parakeet share a dry branch. Named after its 'hoo-po' call, the former has a fan-shaped crest which, when erect, resembles a hand fan with striking black and white zebra stripes. Its nests are untidy, filthy and stink.*

FAR RIGHT *Rose-ringed parakeets are at home in dry, deciduous climates. Flying in noisy flocks, screaming "keeak, keeak" and destroying crops, they waste far more than they can eat. Parakeets live in natural tree hollows.*

WILDLIFE

The oasis of Pushkar offers birds and animals a natural source of life, giving water and food even during the harsh summers as well as providing a habitat to hide in.

LEFT *The large egret is twice the size of the little one and its white, elegant body stands stately on black feet. It makes quick, curious movements with its long flexible neck to get a 360° view of its prey. Its otherwise yellow beak turns black while breeding.*

BELOW *Measured with its tail, the peacock on the acacia is over two-metres long. As India's national bird, the velvety exuberance of its plumes are like eyelet motifs on a rug with cobalt blues and gold-tinged browns. While walking, the peacock carries its tail tautly curved, just off the ground. But when it flies in short spurts, one can see it carry the weight. Gliding down a hill slope is easier and can be done in one graceful sweep.*

BOTTOM *The ashy-brown Indian pond heron is a long-legged wading bird with a pointed beak. Thickset and squat, it has a proportionately shorter neck than other herons. Tucking its head and neck in during its leisurely flight, the pond heron reveals a sudden flash of white wings.*

RIGHT *Tall* sarkanda *grass blossoms by the mountain side.*

FACING PAGE *Black-faced* langurs *with disproportionately long tails.*

ABOVE *The scavenging vultures were a common sight in Rajasthan till a decade ago when they seem to have been mass-obliterated by a fatal disease. These white-backed vultures are striking for their size and wing-span but their bald crests, vicious curved beaks and surpentine necks give them a mean, menacing look. Their large, straggly nests are built daringly on the top of large trees. Just as they jostle and flap over carcasses, they miss no opportunity to bathe, which is possibly why Pushkar pleases them.*

RIGHT *In the grasslands and cultivated areas around Pushkar, the industrious handiwork of the weaver bird is not an infrequent sight. The woven grass tunnel which hangs down from the pendulous, bellow-shaped nest, makes it obligatory for the birds to shoot in their way in full flight – making it predator-proof. The* baya, *or weaver cock, is a polygamist and can father three or four families in different nests built by him.*

The Myth & The Waters

ABOVE *Thundering dauntlessly, the monsoon arrives from the heavens and blesses the landscape with new life, bringing as much joy to the parched fields as to humans, birds, animals and the shrunken lake.*

BELOW *After their ablutions, Rajasthani women present a colourful spectacle on the bathing* ghats.

In the glowing sands of Rajasthan's Thar desert, Pushkar presents a pristine and natural oasis. The Mughal emperor Jahangir admitted to visiting the spot 15 times, merely to gaze upon the lake.

The devout believe that the Sarovar was formed from one of the three petals that dropped off the lotus seat of Brahma (see p. 40). Over the centuries, the sanctity of the spot has been reinforced by the temples that have risen by its banks. Steps lead down in a series of ghats to the purifying water. The white structures reflected in the Mediterranean blue of the lake may recall Greece to the international travellers, but at closer quarters the foliated arches of the *jharokhas* projecting over the water bring them irrevocably back to India.

The *jharokhas* frame stunning views of the lake, where worshippers indulge in ritual baths offering water to their ancestors and pay obeisance to the sun. The ultimate prayer is for moksha, to be released from the endless cycle of rebirth and earthly sorrow. Such spectacles evoke the lives of the ancient sages. They are known to have discarded worldly matters as mere illusion, and sought the meaning of existence in the seclusion of remote forests, deserts and hills. The heat generated by their penance (*tapas*) and austerities gained them the reverence of ordinary mortals immersed in the material world.

The throng that attends the great Pushkar fair is more than willing to live for days under minimal shelter, with perhaps just the sky as a moonlit tent or, at the most, a flimsy construction of bamboo and cloth. The primitive facilities are no cause for distress. The vast waters of the lake are as easily used for ritual as they are for ablutions. Faith, it would seem, builds immunity from disease and even wards off infection!

Exaggerated tales of the depth of the lake at Pushkar still continue. "Foreign scientists came to ascertain the Sarovar's depth," said a young priest, "but all their diving and measuring came to no avail because the water goes down to the centre of the earth." This boast was noted by Jahangir (in *Tuzuk-i-Jahangiri*), whose curiosity for all things was remarkable: "They also believe that the tank is bottomless. After experimentation it became apparent that in no place was it more than twelve ells[1] deep [10 metres]. The perimeter was also measured and found to be nearly a kos[2] and a half [6 kilometres]."

[1] Ell: 83.8 cms
[2] Kos: 4.17 kms

LEFT & ABOVE LEFT *Even today the pilgrimage is a demonstration of how little has changed with the passing centuries. Since ancient times, India has had a tradition of the unstitched garment both for men and women. As metres of white or coloured dhotis and turbans or sarees and* odhnis *are spread out to dry in the sun, visions of that ancient culture reappear again.*

BELOW *While the devout bathe, hoping to achieve their own purposes, tourists at Pushkar have often found them to be a rather photogenic subject. Photography is now strictly forbidden on the ghats with a large and efficient police force to enforce this law. Bathers often take the law into their own hands and confiscate the cameras of voyeurs.*

Apart from the trade in cattle that dates back to antiquity – when barter was the mode – today cows, oxen, camels and horses are vigorously bought and sold in separately demarcated areas. Some visitors to the fair are there only for the experience offered by this vast congregation of humanity and animals, while others return year after year for peace and relaxation that the place and its interaction with the local people offer.

Rules govern the use of the ghats – unspoken, unwritten and age-old – with different castes and communities bathing in their traditional spaces. As dusk falls, sadhus build bonfires by the ghats, as smoke from their *chillums* conjures for them visions of other worlds and other lives.

RIGHT *There are not many societies in the world where traditional garments like the dhoti can be worn both by the head of state and captains of industry without any qualms. Nor is the saree out of place today by the village well, at an international bankers' meet or on the fashion ramps of the world. Most of India's fashion continues unperturbed by the colour forecasts and colour ways of Indian designers who have gradually become trendsetters and tailors to the world. In rural and urban Rajasthan, all the colours of the rainbow always seem to be in vogue. The presence of tourists with cameras must somewhat constrict the freedom of the bathers today. Rousselet describes a different scene in 1878. "A bevy of young girls, covered merely with gauze veils, disport themselves in the lake, in front of the temples of Krishna, God of Love, making the shores resound with their fresh ringing laughter; and when from time to time they pause in their sport, and rise out of the waves, with their hair streaming over their bare shoulders, one might easily take them for the beautiful 'Apsaras' who were, able to charm the divine Brahma."*

FACING PAGE TOP *The Akali Nihangs, a colourful and more orthodox sect of the Sikhs, throng to Pushkar to pray at their gurudwara. Guru Nanak is believed to have bathed here, and Guru Gobind Singh vsited Pushkar in 1705. This also gives them an opportunity to communicate and dialogue with holy men of other sects who congregate by the ghats.*

FACING PAGE TOP LEFT *"Please Respect The Hindu Religion..." the notice board reads for foreigners, but cricket seems as assimilated as the local* gulli-danda. *After the national success of the film* Lagaan, *cricket matches are now arranged in the* mela *grounds of Pushkar between visiting foreigners and the local participants at the fair. What was exported as a county sport from England, has now hijacked India into becoming its national sport. Two young Brahmans, disregarding the rules of conduct which are numbered and enumerated in yellow at the ghats, turn Pushkar into their private stadium. As the game of bat and ball proceeds on the sacred ghats, the ritual of cricket seems to have been accepted both by the Brahmans and the pantheon of Indian gods.*

BELOW *Considered by some as an essential part of spiritual fitness, physical exercise is rigorously practised in the* akharas *and on the banks of Pushkar's sacred* Sarovar.

EPHEMERAL PUSHKAR

Commerce & Cattle

ABOVE *The original manuscript of poetry of Naraharidas lies at the Charan Sahitya Shodh Sansthan, Ajmer. This had played a very crucial role for Hindus, helping with the ban of cow slaughter in Akbar's time.*

COWS

In the Vedas, cow worship came to be associated with the earth goddess. Today, she is commonly called as Gau Mata or Gaiyya Ma, her milk cherished much as a baby would its mother's. She also helped to add to the cattle wealth, the measure of riches for the pastoral people. It is for this reason that milch cows were called *aghanya* (non-slayable).

In an early 20th-century oleograph, the belief that each part of the cow's body is the abode of a god, has been literally represented. This version is a take-off from older versions where Kamadhenu, the magical wish-fulfilling cow of plenty mentioned in the Puranas, is similarly depicted. An interesting tale from the 17th century recounts how poetry motivated Akbar to reconsider the slaying of cows: The poet Barhath Naraharidas, a resident of Pushkar, went to Akbar's court where he was given an audience. The poet confessed that he had no work with the emperor, but some cows did! Akbar was intrigued and when some cows were ushered in with placards around their necks, the poet demanded permission to translate their language for the emperor. These three couplets so moved Akbar that cow-slaughter was banned in his kingdom. Translated they read:

If an enemy holds a blade of grass in the mouth, no one will kill him in battle.
We cows only graze grass, so where is the question of killing us?
To Hindus we do not offer milk as elixir nor do we give poison to Muslims
The bulls we give birth to as sons, please everyone's hearts
Says poet Naraharidas, O Lord of Delhi, the cows fold their hands and ask
What fault is it of ours that we are killed? Even in death our leather gives you shoes.

PRECEDING PAGES *Seen from the creator's viewpoint, the graphic shadows of the awkward camels seem to take the forms of tribal art.*

If the majority of the cattle traded at Pushkar was to decide its name, traditionally it should have been called a bull or cow fair. Comparative statistics show that the Nagaur bulls are the most sought-after transaction since they are used for both ploughing and breeding. They were in demand roughly thrice more than the camel. However, the camel and the dune complete both the reality and the cliché of Rajasthan. It is, nevertheless, curious that of the few sheep, goats and donkeys – of which 1, 29 and 10 are recorded as having been brought for sale between 1996 and 2000 – not one was sold. In the same time span, the total proceeds from the sale of cattle was Rs 4,670,400 and Rs 5,618,300, and the government earned revenues of Rs 173,843 and Rs 255,809 respectively.

RIGHT *A popular oleograph from the Ravi Varma Press of the early 20th century shows the Cow of 84 Divinities. "O Arya people!" the caption above reads, "Protect the cow or protect the stomach." The man who waves his arms standing before the cow says, "Do not kill it. The cow is everybody's life," while a dark man, clad only in a dhoti, pours milk to people of different religions: Hindus, a Muslim, a Parsi and a Christian. The foreigner in striped trousers seems an obvious target of this propaganda for the text near him reads, "Give me milk – Sahib."*

Although the bull was among the first animals in India to have a prominent cult of its own from as early as the Indus Valley Civilization (circa 2800-1900 BCE), it has been pointed out that the cow finally took its place in the Vedic period. At Pushkar, the decrease in transactions of the bovine family is also related to the fact that the Nagaur cattle fair held in February each year draws the largest crowds for this specialized purchase.

Broadly, there are five breeds of indigenous cows which are transacted at Pushkar. The first is the noble Gir cow, whose home is the western tracts of India – including north Maharashtra, Gujarat south of the Kathiawar peninsula up to Kutch, and western Rajasthan – and can be easily

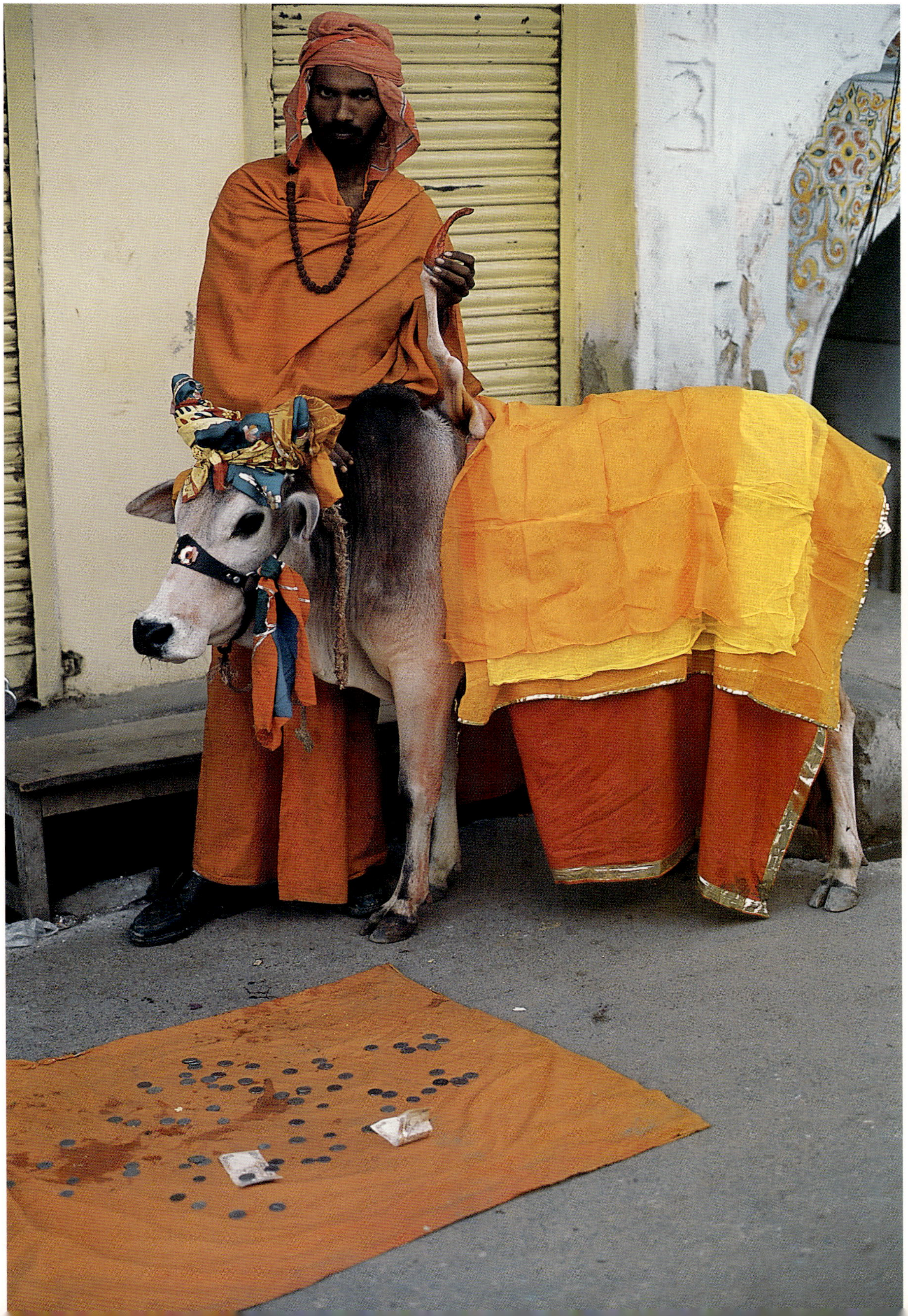

LEFT *A Kalbelia from the snake charmers' community, dressed up as a sadhu, waits patiently for soft-hearted pilgrims. The painted cow, adorned in tinsel-edged fabric and a peacock feather between its horns, aligns itself as one dear to the cowherd god Krishna. Just its sight is enough for a devout Hindu to give a coin or two. Some cows are even trained to answer questions on the future by nodding the head in different ways. It is quite another matter that Brahmans don't seem to object since the Kalbelia makes his earnings disguised as one of them, and that he will return home and eat just about anything he or his family find in the jungle from a peacock to all sorts of wild animals.*

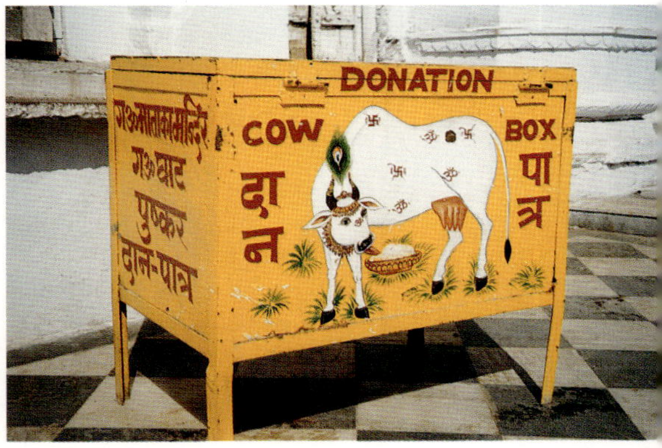

ABOVE *The slit in the "Cow Donation Box" needs no other explanation. Everywhere in Pushkar, the cow and its images are used to earn money. The daily importance of the cow in India can also be ascertained from the following statistics. According to the 2001 census, 10 percent of India uses dried cow dung cakes as cooking fuel. Midget cows, or those with deformities are considered even more unique and awesome for begging alms.*

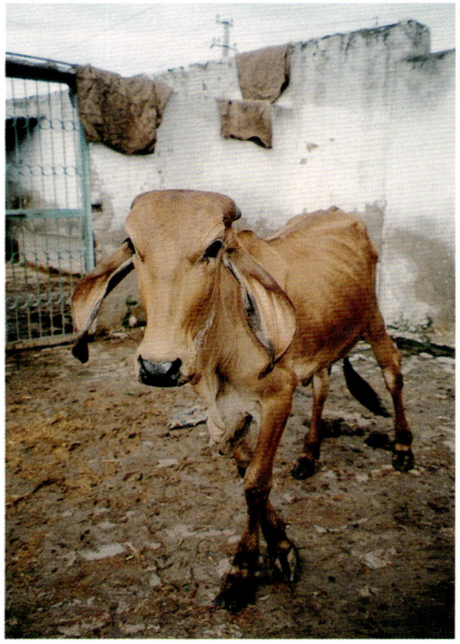

TOP & ABOVE *A young Gir cow, with its large flapping ears, being raised at the Kashyap Dairy in Vaishali, Ajmer. It has yet to grow its conspicuous handlebar horns which will give it an air of aristocracy. This large-horned cow is called a* 'rindi'*, whereas one with downward pointing horns resembling the okra vegetable is called a* 'bhindi' *cow.*

recognized by its large horns which curve out symmetrically like a grand handle-bar moustache. Normally of light salmon colour, Gir cows have large, downward pointing ears, a prominent hump and well developed udders with a mild yield. These are exported to Brazil and the Americas. The Gir bullock, though slow, is heavy and powerful and used in western India to grade the local cattle and produce breeds like the Mewati, Nimari and Deoni with shorter curved horns. Gir, in Gujarat, is better known as the last reserve of the Asian lion.

The white Nagauri cows and bulls are slimmer and more athletic. Although native to the areas near Pushkar – Karkeri, Babaicha, Narwar – they largely belong to the Jodhpur region and have been cross-bred with the Haryana and Kankrej breeds. They have straight horns and ears parallel to the ground with a somewhat alert look.

The Rathi breed, named after a Jat clan, wear dark grey markings on the head while the body is white, mottled brown, or grey. A flat forehead leads to a straight face, large white eyes, short pendulous ears, small lateral horns. a moderate hump and a short tail with a black switch. They are powerful for their medium build, with well-developed forequarters.

Tharparkar or Thari, the fourth breed, comes from Hyderabad, Pakistan (Thar-par-kar which means 'across the Thar desert'). A medium-sized bovine with a white-to-grey body coat, the oxen are fine draught animals, while the cows provide good milk. The Tharis have spread from Marwar in the east to Kutch in the west, down to Palanpur and the north of Mumbai, but the purest ones come from Amarkot and Nauket.

Thick long horns, worn like the crown of a tribal king, distinguish the Kankrej bulls and cows. They hold up their neck with an arrogance and their nostrils seem to swell with pride. Their shaded greys, from silver to iron with a steely black shine, is a familiar sight from the coastal Rann of Kutch to Ahmedabad where they originate; they are now very popular in Rajasthan. In Brazil, they call them *'guzrat'* supplanting the 'j' with the more familiar 'z' of their own country.

Rohtak, Hissar and Jind in Haryana, Nabha and Patiala in the Punjab lead the milk market with their heavy, jet-black buffaloes whose tails, faces, and extremities have white markings. However, in the various animal competitions organized by the government authorities at Pushkar, the prize for the maximum amount of milk usually goes to the mottled black-and-white Holstein breed of cows. These were originally raised in Friesland in the northern Netherlands, before the Danish Duchy of Holsteins gave them its name.

Beginning with the Christian era, popular Hinduism was propagated through mythological works known as the Puranas. These elaborated upon the Vedic idea of the sacredness of the cow. One of the stories has it that the cow was born on the same day as Brahma, the Creator. By extension, killing a cow was declared to be as heinous a sin as killing a Brahman.

The *Kartik* full moon in October-November, when the annual pilgrimage and cattle fair take place at Pushkar, is also the auspicious date for *vrisha-utsarga*, when a bull is stamped with the trident of Shiva, or any other auspicious symbol, and then freed to ensure good breeding and fertility among the cattle of the community. The 12th bright half of *Kartik* is also one of the two auspicious days of the calendar when the Puranas recommend the worship of the cow.

According to ancient charters, no living thing is allowed to be put to death within the limits of Pushkar (*Rajputana Gazetteer*, Vol II). In the famine conditions of 2002, the government took upon itself to supply fodder, but it seemed an impossible and thankless job to be able to do so. Many of the participants were compelled to leave behind their unsold cows and calves in the *mela* grounds to be carried away by butchers. The participants felt that at least the sin of a cow's death was not directly on their hands!

LEFT *Not much seems to have changed in the Rajasthani landscape since Vedic times. Cows and oxen still symbolize wealth, though they may not always mean cash flow in the trying times which constant droughts bring about.*

BELOW *While young priests wait for clients, called* yajaman *(the one who performs the sacrifice), whom they will assist in their prayers and bathing rituals – a "Save the Cow" medallion campaigns against the slaughtering of this divine bovine.*

	1911		1996		2000	
	ATTENDED	SOLD	ATTENDED	SOLD	ATTENDED	SOLD
Cows & Bullocks	14,543	6253	4,249	2,813	4,905	2,829
Buffaloes	–	–	1,149	773	1,284	420
Camels	4,607	2,649	11,735	4,413	1,167	768
Horses	970	462	2,030	1,084	13,981	6,822

LEFT & BELOW *A Holstein cow which produced 34 kgs of milk in one day to win the milch cow of the year 2002 award being bathed on the sands (below), while two other contenders (left) graze on scanty straw in the famine year of 2002 when fodder was brought from the Punjab. Danish, Prussian, German, Indian – the cows remain unfazed about their geographical origins, while a signboard in the distance reads,* "Sar dard ko goli maro: Saridon" *(Shoot the headache in the head) – or leave the headaches for the humans, as the cows would perhaps interpret it!*

ABOVE *Camels neck and kiss using each other for a gentle scratch.*

PRECEDING PAGES *The classic silhouettes of Pushkar's twilight which unite man and animal, always become its most cliched representation and memory.*

BELOW *A cavalcade of camels return from grazing at dusk* (godhuli)*, when dust is raised by the cows. Their silhouettes glide like a shadow play with cut-outs, an eternal act on a biblical landscape. Their walk may seem awkward and ungainly, but camels are ideally fashioned for the desert. A 'vacuum' within each hoof prevents even a heavily burdened beast from sinking into the loose sand.*

CAMELS

Pushkar displays the one-humped Arabian camel *(Camelus dromedaries)*. The Latin name is what creates the confusion for people, who variously call the animal a camel or dromedary, whereas the term camel by itself refers to the *Camelus bactrianus*, or Bactrian camel with two humps on the back for storing its food. Native originally to Chinese Turkestan, this was domesticated for carrying loads in Manchuria. Genetically, it is also related to the llamas, alpacas and vicunas of South America.

The camels arrive imaginatively sheared and tattooed to participate in the festivities. Since camel herds of the same breed and stock are not easy to distinguish – some traditional tattoos called *kheeng* have been evolved. These help herders identify their camels with ease. Black henna, or ink, is normally used for the identification marks, but the Rabaris or Raikas make permanent marks with the handles of large ladles heated on fire. These marks, combined with *moondra* – the decorative motifs cut out of their hair – give each camel a unique look of its own. Added to these are the personalized or regional fashions for the saddlery and trappings of his herd which remain the choice of each camel owner.

The 'ship of the desert' can survive in the wild without a rider. But once it has a rider, it describes and announces his status. While men make the saddles and harnesses, the weaving and embroidery for the camel regalia is usually done by the women of each household. What cannot be domestically manufactured is bought from the cattle fairs

A camel's face, reminiscent of the extinct animals of paleontology, is decorated around its gaping wide mouth and its eternally-distended nostrils, with neck bands, *soria and mohra*, made of

What the beggar is in England, the Faqueer is in India; with the difference, that whereas the former is considered next akin to a vagrant, and (though often deserving of the alms which he solicits) is held in the very lowest esteem, the latter, taking religious devotion as the apparent basis of his conduct, is not only tolerated as a privileged member of society (imposter would be a better word), but is, on account of his prescribed austerities, even regarded with honour and respect. These Faqueers are, in many instances, sad rogues, and very immoral. Religion for such is merely a cloak for every species of wickedness. Some coat themselves over with all kinds of filth, and in consequence become objects of disgust. Some there are who, completely wrapped up in the benighting folds of idolatory, with fervency and zeal undertake and perform penances which excite our wonder, hoping thereby to ensure for themselves endless happiness in heaven.

— CHARLES RICHARD FRANCIS

When bicycles are no good in the sand, they must be parked and forsaken for the 'ship of the desert'. The business of hiring out camels is rather flexible: by the hour, by the day or by the week. "Gopal's Camel Agencies" reads a board, as the short-tempered and grumpy Ajmal Baba temporarily occupies the chair of the proprietor. He curses all the passers-by, who smile and do not answer back. In the broad understanding of life, Hindus accept his abuses, interpreting them as blessings.

RIGHT *The best-dressed camel award is won each year by Ashok Shivani Tak, who calls himself a camel decorator. He is a keen collector of the finest camel trappings, old saddles and textiles.*

BELOW & BOTTOM *The dung of the camel is collected, spread and dried before being used as fuel to cook food.*

rope and leather and coloured embroidery and ropes, known as *belcha*. The long, awkward neck gives plenty of space to hang an elaborate necklace of heavy, coloured cotton ropes strung and woven in a net of beads, mirrored embroidery bands, cowries, seashells – once used as currency – a brass *chaurasi* and bells. A traditional Rajasthani song goes, "*Mahro gorbandh nakhralo*" (my camel necklace demands its own attention). Below the belly, hangs a *jhul* with colourful woven strappings. On the ankles of the front legs are worn jingling *nevri*.

The camel saddle is a many-layered affair. The first is a *melkhuri*, a layer of wool or thick cotton placed on the animal's back, followed by four *singharas* and then a four-point saddle cloth called *chheuti* which is usually embroidered or patched with motifs. The wooden saddle, or *kathi* – normally covered with a brass sheet in open cutwork – is attached to leather cushions, or *tharas*. A round pommel on the saddle provides a handle. This is tied on the camel's stomach with sheep wool straps – *tang* – hung with dangling stirrups called *pagras*.

With so many animals tethered to pegs, carts and each other, it is not easy to make the best buy, leave alone see all the mobile merchandise. But fortunately, Kishan Lal, a Rajput Rao from the village of Bhagega of Neem ka Thana in Sikar, came forward to explain how he, as one of the large buyers and sellers, would choose his purchase. "There are nine large and nine small things to watch out for," he explained "while buying a dromedary, especially among the light fleet ones which are reared and trained for riding."

A sitting camel's tail is often pulled to see its state of health. Should it stick out its tongue or make a noise, it should not be bought. A healthy camel is normally expected to jerk and stand up.

RIGHT *A buyer inspects a camel for large, healthy teeth.*

BELOW *A checklist of negative and positive attributes for buying a camel, based on its large and small parts.*

WHAT SHOULD BE LARGE/LONG/THICK/STRONG/WIDE

1 AANKH eyes (and with light)
2 DAANTAVAL teeth
3 GARDAN neck (as also thick)
4 THUA hump
5 NAAD base of neck
6 CHHAATI chest
7 BELA body
8 PINDA thigh
9 AASAN seat

WHAT SHOULD BE SMALL

a MOOH face
b KAAN ears (and shapely)
c IKRI elbow
d GATTA sole to ankle
e PANDI sole (and round)
f IDAR space between front legs
g GAIL KA AASAN seat behind hump
h POONCHH tail
i MUTANA genitals

GOATS & SHEEP

Even though goats and sheep are not transacted at Pushkar, they are very much a part of the landscape of Rajasthan. "It isn't easy transporting a herd of goats," a farmer explained, "whereas you can ride your way to Pushkar with a camel herd."

Goats provide a poor man's milk and a rich man's diet. Rajasthani species of goat breed twice a year, making them a sought-after and lucrative commercial proposition.

While a goat's ears are cut for beauty or for 'show' – a word the herders use in English to express themselves better in Rajasthani – randy young rams are obliged to have their genitals tied with a rope lest they impregnate goats which are less than two years old.

BELOW *The patch-brown,* parbatsari *goat named after the area of its origins. The plain, red one called* telia *is from Pali, while the long-haired ones are from Jaisalmer and Barmer.*

FAR LEFT *A young ram, its genitals tied with a rope, lest it impregnate another goat which is not ready to breed.*

LEFT *A goat's ears are cut to enhance its beauty, or so the farmers believe.*

FAR LEFT *Sheared sheep look emaciated in the sandy landscape where the rains turn even the dunes into a jungle of shrubs.*

LEFT *Travelling on foot with the goats is a slow business, especially for a disbanded herd. Here, a goat rides a camel cart.*

In the past, animal sacrifices were in vogue. Fortunately, today the gods and goddesses are considered to be less blood-thirsty. At Pushkar, goats are now offered symbolically and a copper ring is pierced into the ear. They are then called *amria*, possibly from *amar*, eternal, for no one is supposed to kill them. Much like the humped bulls, they grow into large rams and roam free. Shepherds use their services for breeding, but nowadays public moral standards are not always observed and even the *amria* rams are consumed as meat.

LEFT *Even during the monsoon when the hills are green, a saddle black goat leaps precariously to stretch for a few green leaves.*

Baba Balak Das Ghodewala of Ramsar, renowned for his white, unblemished Nukra horses, shares a moment of affection with one of them. The mottled horses may look beautiful, he points out, but everyone wants to mate their mares with his stallions. "I charge Rs 5,100 per shagun," he boasts.

HORSES

In Hindu mythology, Brahma is linked to the horse as its Creator. This original winged white horse was kept hidden in the Ksheer Sagar, the celestial ocean of milk. Its name was Uchchhaihshravas and its neighing is believed to be a nasal mystery called the *anusvara* which, when chanted with a seed syllable, makes a mantra imperishable. Walker writes that, "The *anusvara*, correctly intoned, is said to set up cerebral vibrations and interior echoes of irresistible potency." Because the horse is not indigenous to India, it was treasured as a novelty and a status symbol. The fact that bridegrooms in several parts of India still arrive at the bride's house on horseback is linked to this special status.

The high prices which horses still fetch at Pushkar, in a century of machines and automation, is possibly a momentum from this past. The most expensive horse exhibited at Pushkar in 2002 was for Rs 1.2 million, roughly 40 times that of the highest priced camel. This price was totally disproportionate to the service provided by the animal, but was explained as a premium for pure, breeding horses only.

It is interesting that Brahma should also be associated in mythology with the first horse sacrifice called *ashvamedha yajna*. It is also interesting to note that Brahma's Pushkar is also historically connected to the last recorded horse sacrifice performed in India by Maharaja Jai Singh II of Jaipur around 1727 (see p. 52). A horse breeder at Pushkar shows his entry pass where each animal is obliged to be registered with the fair authorities. Only when the *ravaana*, or departure, is officially announced can all the animals leave. This is done to ensure the presence of animals during the Pushkar fair, so that the tourists can also see all the camels, horses, cows and buffaloes.

ABOVE & BELOW *A large, green* neem *tree shades a small temple to Ramdev-ji, revered all across Rajasthan. Oxen and cows surround this temple during the cattle fair. At other times of the year, its status reverts to a roadside shrine. On the right farmers scramble for the free fodder distributed during a drought year.*

ABOVE, RIGHT & BELOW *The Kathiawari breed, easily recognized by its alert inward-turned ears which meet at the tips, is prized over the mixed breeds. Their palette includes chestnut, dapple grey, dun, flea-bitten grey and the classic black Marwari.*

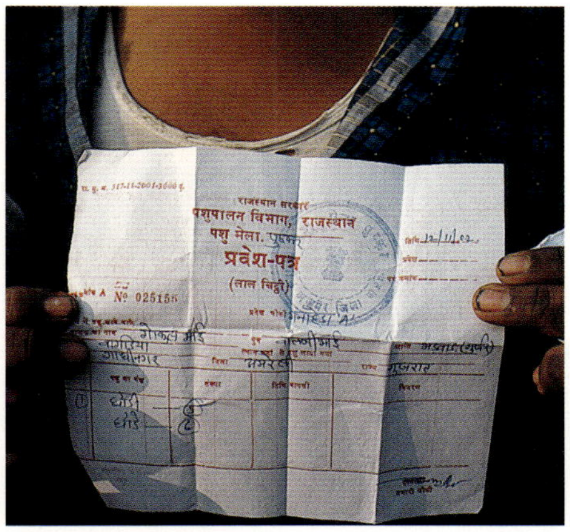

ABOVE *A herder shows his ravaana, or exit paper.*

LEFT *Jean Marc of Quebec is now called Mark Gopal after 25 years in India. Married to a woman from Andhra Pradesh, he and his three children live in Pushkar where he breeds Kathiawari horses and teaches horse riding. He is not alone as there is an Italian couple who live in a village nearby.*

BELOW *A rebellious colt is being trained or 'run in' before a backdrop of the turning ferris wheels.*

The silhouette of the Ganga Mai Temple of the Rehgar Samaj and its fortified wall light up on the horizon. The three arched gates of the Pushkar mela *grounds can be seen in the foreground.*

ABOVE *Folk dancers in traditional costumes watch the other performers.*

ABOVE RIGHT *Running the matka race with a terracotta pitcher full of water, provides added thrills when participants crash into each other.*

RIGHT & FAR RIGHT *Students taking part in a race and displaying their acrobatic skills.*

BELOW & FACING PAGE BOTTOM *The tug-of-war game between tourists and the locals is a popular event, with much cheering for both teams.*

ABOVE *Turbaned villagers watch their women play tug-of-war, using skills perfected while pulling ropes to collect well water.*

ABOVE LEFT *Liveried camels and their owners march in a procession.*

LEFT & FAR LEFT *A Rajasthani proudly displays his prize-winning long moustache.*

FOLLOWING PAGES *An aerial view of large circus tents and ferris wheels records the carnival atmosphere of the fair.*

TOP ROW *At night, the Rajasthan Tourism Development Corporation organizes dance and music performances of better-known forms. The Tehra Tali dancers from Pali (left), sit with cymbals attached to their arms to perform a daring act of rhythmic movements with open swords held between their teeth. Kishangarh's Chari dancers (right) with brass 'fire' pots on their heads.*

FACING PAGE & BELOW *Chakri dancers from Kota enchant and swirl in their colourful skirts.*

BOTTOM ROW *Fire eaters put up their own impressive performance where fire clouds pour out of their mouths before bewildered audiences.*

Watching faces (here and preceding pages) can be a fascinating pursuit at Pushkar, displaying a mix of all the races who have mingled in Rajasthan.

RIGHT *The popular Indian sport of* kabaddi *keeps the two teams as alert as the audience, which shares all the emotions of the physical touch-and-run across the middle line along with the grappling and wrestling.*

BELOW *This toy plane at Pushkar makes child's play of diplomacy and shows how a China Airlines body and an Air India tail fin can take two nations speeding ahead in cooperation.*

LEFT *Gigantic wheels put a new scale to the fair's skyline. But the afternoon sees a moment of lull for the ferris wheels, when both the owners and the visitors stop to eat and indulge in a siesta.*

BELOW *Exhausted after showing and seeing the merchandise of cattle, three farmers settle down in the winter sun and call it half-a-day.*

The Bazaars

The very mention of the word 'bazaar' already sets up expectations. Appropriated from its Persian origin to evoke a row of Oriental shops spilling merchandise, it was a word the English language could hardly do without in its colonizing phase. The regimented order suggested by the Western market place was perhaps too tame and predictable to capture such an evocative and stirring image for the 19th-century travellers.

If you went further from the Orientalist version of the Middle-Eastern bazaars, adding to that image the rich eclecticism of India and the colours of a Rajasthani street, the picture would

ABOVE *Clock arms and the sun's rays dominate the tower of Shri Surya* dharamshala. *Many impressive buildings built by royal families, traders and industrialists as guest houses, have been turned into shops on the main street of Sadar Bazaar.*

BELOW *In the shadow of the Papmochini Temple, a river of colour flows continuously during the Pushkar fair.*

come close to that in Pushkar. But this image would begin to burst at its frame only by a walk down the streets of Pushkar when the cattle fair, pilgrimage and *mela* combine, and a sea of humanity flows through the same streets.

The serpentine Sadar Bazaar of Pushkar begins wherever you are game. Many arterial streets lead on to this main street, which is also used by pilgrims on their sacred circumambulations. You will meet the priests before you know it, for they have an eagle eye for their 'prey'. You will meet the smooth-talking touts, the instant money-changers and the young motorbike boys who sell hotel rooms with views and terraces to smoke on and cuisines so diverse, you would imagine yourself to be in a gourmet capital.

FACING PAGE BOTTOM *Ram Dyal-ji Maharaj of Shahpura, renowned for his* path *of the Bhagwad, being paraded through Pushkar's Sadar Bazaar. After its reading, the Bhagwad is held over the head as a form of respect and carried in a procession.*

INDIAN
CIRCUS

Dr.
PEARCING

YOGA
PAINTER KIKASSO
KIKASSO
YNTRA
PALMIST
TANTRIK PAINTER
KIKASSO
YOGA

BAZAAR BIZARRE

What is it you did or didn't
want?
Lenin by the wave of a wand ?
Hat for the head, pillow for your
bed, water for the throat
Bells for a goat
Batteries, postcards, rolls of film
Shampoos, soaps for every skin
To wash at Pushkar all your sins
Massage from head to toe
bone crack for a friend or foe
Gems, jewels, silver, gold
Designer, copied, or very old
Scissors, tweezers, plaited hair
And pointed bras if you dare
Music of the world on test
At the tabla east beats west
Latin beans, reggae jeans
Clothes for middle aged teens
Backless frontless printed plain
Lurex hand tie-dyed or stained
Get a skirt with thousand pleats
Pink and yellow Indian sweets
Malpuas as a must, topped with a
rabri crust
Israeli Chinese Italian
As much as your belly can
Pushkar rose petal paste
Curries spiced to your taste
But weigh yourself before you eat
To let your fortune card repeat
Why enter the rat race
When you can live at Pushkar
pace?

TOP & ABOVE *A host of hairdressers and masseurs line the streets but the one above includes "Bone Crack" – a special treat (the man has turbo powered hands)!*

RIGHT *"No Naice No Pay OK!" A simple sincerity in the old marketing confidence of promising 'satisfaction or money back' lures tired tourists.*

FACING PAGE *Age-old gods, new titans and fallen icons of the 20th century such as Lenin – all hang equal at a shop for tourist handicrafts.*

The Nimaj Temple rents its unused frontage for temporary shops which spring up during the mela. This one sells colourful parandis *which adorn women's hair. Its indiscreet display of bras which dance in the breeze, do not deter the orthodox, even veiled women from asking for them.*

What were once homes have now succumbed to the lure of commercialization on their ground floors. The landlords now live in the comparative peace of the first floor. If there is a view of Pushkar's lake from the upper floors, the owners move away making place for tourists.

Although there are unwritten demarcations within the bazaars which separate the fruit and vegetable vendors from the dentist (right) and blacksmiths, an interesting element of surprise constantly hangs in the air. Saddlery sells next to ceremonial spears or rubber toys next to chequered woollen blankets. To add to this, mobile vendors accost buyers with a bewilderment of merchandise.

ABOVE *An art emporium adds its own sense of surrealism to Salvador Dali by first planting his portrait in the desert town of Pushkar and then by using Hebrew for the signage.*

LEFT *Even Dracula would be honoured to know that an enterprising salesman can earn a living by impersonating him on the streets of Pushkar.*

FAR LEFT *As hard technology works its recurring instant wonder, the Internet, a Pushkar-style department store on Sadar Bazar, is undeterred from marketing "All Kind [of] General Things That You Think, You Dream...!"*

FAR LEFT BOTTOM *The world's merchandise seems to be available in Pushkar from imported shampoos to peanut butter to film. Some of the supplies come from the young tourists themselves.*

FACING PAGE FAR LEFT *The makers of Saridon, the panacea for headaches, frame one of the streets with a gateway. No urban visitor in Pushkar can imagine that even the healthy, carefree villagers could have a headache.*

Pilgrims perform the circumambulation, literally crossing 'the bridge' between their reality and their aspirations.

ABOVE *A safer White House hidden in Pushkar.*

ABOVE RIGHT & FACING PAGE TOP *The Royal Tents of Jodhpur pitched at Ganahera. A staff member manually replaces water for the flushes.*

RIGHT *The rock band Pink Floyd would be as zapped as their listeners, were they to arrive in Pushkar and see how their name adds to India's time warp.*

BELOW *Shiva's third eye is flaunted as the name of a restaurant, unaware that should the god choose to open it, the world would be destroyed. Reading the signage at Pushkar can be amusing as one hunts for "Brack-fast" or "Deener".*

FACING PAGE BOTTOM *The magically-lit pool of the Pushkar Resort holds an Arabian Night's appeal for its residents who arrive after all their senses have been almost assaulted by the sights, sounds and touch of Pushkar. Located only 3 kilometres away, it makes a calm counterpoint to the eternal happening which Pushkar has become.*

receptivity. During the short camel fair when hotels charge special rates, the tents can be a memorable experience. The Royal Tents of Jodhpur pitched at Ganahera and a host of others, put guests close to the clean brown sands of Pushkar. For those seeking peace, the Pushkar Resort at Motisar is an oasis of calm which also falls outside the 'vegetarian' limit of the pilgrimage. Closer lies the Jagat Singh Palace, a 'palace' reconstituted from the remains of demolished structures of Marwar.

Long-staying backpackers have a large choice of rooms overlooking the lake, while some prefer more bucolic accommodation away on the outskirts among the rose fields of the garden-ashrams.

The signages addressed to foreigners are particularly amusing since many of the boards in English are either phonetically spelt or translated from Hindi. Wandering around Pushkar looking out for Dr Pearcing – should you want your ears or nose pierced – or suddenly discovering that another White House exists without the danger of a terrorist attack and with the added attraction of a 'magic garden' attached, must still be one of the wonders of travel in this part of the world.

If one can scratch the surface, look through all religions and rituals, past all the mess that man may have made at Pushkar, and wind one's way quietly before sunset to a lonely stair, on some forgotten ghat – across the tube-lit ones – one can see the lamps being lit and floated on those eternal waters where time has rippled over centuries. One will hear the loud bells, softly from a distance, as the evening *arti* rises to a crescendo. One may wish the loudspeakers away, but the sky will eventually swallow up all that sound. Once one connects to the vastness of nature, one may say as did Eric Newby when he saw the Ganga with his wife: "We both experienced that feeling which comes so rarely to human beings, of wishing that the moment in which we were living might be infinitely prolonged."

ABOVE *The Sai Baba of Shirdi in Maharashtra, whose mass following continues in his second incarnation as the Sai Baba of Whitefields near Bangalore, here lends his name and blessings to a Sai Baba Restaurant.*

RIGHT *A fresco of the temples and ghats, painted by a foreign guest, serves as an unusual backdrop in the Wonderland Restaurant.*

LEFT & BELOW *The renowned ice cream of Ahmedabad – Vadilal – finds a match for its logo and house colours in the vibrant clothes worn by the Kalbelia women enjoying a cup of tea. Traditionally snake charmers, the bold and daring women of this tribe are now better known for their dancing skills or for painting henna motifs on the palms of tourists.*

The Magic of the Time Warp

Pushkar presents a raw, self-confident quality that is simultaneously carnival-like and chaotic, natural and surreal, absurd yet logical to the Indian eye. James Bond-style dark glasses are worn with the same aplomb as the ancient turban. A 'softy' ice cream is enjoyed with as much relish as a betel leaf. Buses in blinding hues race across the tawny desert landscape.

India irons out an extraordinary number of time warps each minute of the day. Undeterred and innocent of the incongruities of their existence, people play out their lives, each a cinematograph that rolls on without direction or apparent structure.

To a visitor from another culture, one who is sensitive and not just critical towards the living theatre that is India, at every street corner the curtain rises to another unpredictable act. It is all a happening and an installation all at once. And constantly. But this is not so for the Indian pilgrims who have a mission at Pushkar. They are part of the act – on stage, so to say – praying, bathing, buying. While they have no reluctance to let anyone or everyone be part of their moving circus, they still need to buy a ticket and visit the many circuses which are on show during the Pushkar fair.

What is it that a pilgrim at Pushkar perceives of in the whole gamut of activity happening around him or her? The deep-rooted religious values broadly divide people into practitioners of *pravrittidharma*, the idea of 'rolling on', of Karmic action which runs the 'three worlds', which are moving and non-moving, as the Mahabharata puts it. Everyone living their life according to *pravritti* must return to the world on its terms and shall be obliged to act in conformity. But the other option exists, equally. Those who choose to practice *nivrittidharma*, or renounce the world, must recognize only their own self-imposed

limits. They can abandon this circus of life and become foresters. No one looks at them as marginalized. On the contrary, they are revered. As the Brihadaranyaka Upanishad points out, they are on their "path leading to the gods" (*devayana*) while all the lesser mortals are simply on their "path leading to the fathers" (*pitrayana*). The latter will be born again and again. So how can they step out of life, observe themselves, pass a value judgement on what they already know and fully accept at face value? Their circus must lie elsewhere where it is being artificially enacted for them: by midgets and monkeys, acrobats and magicians. At Pushkar, because it is a holy pilgrimage, both the householder and the forester can, and do, meet. This interaction of saint and sinner throws up its own incongruities.

Westerners who are immediately perceptive of the multiple layers of existence/acceptance in India, cross the line easily and become a natural part of the act. Others, forever making comparisons and listing the differences, fall into the judgemental trap. However incredible India is, it can still disappoint them. They have made the fundamental mistake of carting their measures as part of their daily baggage. India does not seek their condescension, nor can such an ancient culture in momentum be expected to make amends for them at every step.

For over five millennia now, the land of this subcontinent has churned everyone who has come and ground them into its own millstone to produce a taste of rich and varied spices – sweet, sour, chilly, salty, bitter, pungent – all from the six tastes of a true Indian experience.

What may seem a time warp in other worlds lies here harmoniously ironed out in a blend

ABOVE *Pictures such as these, continue to click in the mind. Tourists pose before a painted curtain of Shri Pushkar Raj, 'king' of all Indian pilgrimages.*

FACING PAGE *Tradition and modernity marry easily at Pushkar. Fabrics, bright with natural dyes, reflect the electrifying colours of buses, while a vanilla cone merges well with the antique design of silver jewellery and the classic upturned moustache.*

PAGES 154-155 *Men impersonate women in the instant entertainment provided to passers-by. The backdrop shows circus stunt women.*

murmuring
BIRD
Cruel

ABOVE *Iron works which are collapsible and mobile, are carried from fair to fair by an enterprising entertainer from Madhya Pradesh. His banner is of the Taj Mahal – the universally acceptable 'national symbol'.*

BELOW *A street actor impersonates a female character against a backdrop depicting a magic show.*

ABOVE & LEFT *The Indian circus in a village scenario still continues to represent many of the people's aspirations. If wild animals represent control over the dangers of the jungle; heroic acts of speeding motorcycles dare technology and defy the laws of gravity; women dressed in Western attire evoke the foreign lands; while dwarfs and acrobats continue the traditional profession of the itenerant nats who still set up their props in a village, perform and travel on.*

ABOVE *Stuck in the sand, a tractor driver revs up the engine as the front wheels rise in the air like a rebellious galloping horse.*

RIGHT *At the November full moon* mela, *the post-lunch sunshine puts even the alert Rajasthan police into a siesta mode.*

ABOVE *The collapsible 21st-century Maruti showroom now seen at Pushkar which reads, "My Dream, my Maruti."*

LEFT & BELOW LEFT *Overloading is part of the joy, both for the transport companies which run in the rural areas earning more revenue, and for the travellers who often prefer the open ride of the roof rather than the warm, constricting interior.*

BELOW *A vehicle is almost a mobile home and it offers many advantages over plodding camel carts.*

THE ENVIRONS

Hotel Jannat

BELOW *A 19th-century etching by Capt J Luard. The 'Might of Islam' mosque in Delhi, was built from the material of 26 destroyed Hindu and Jain temples. Ibn Batuta, the Arab historian, recorded in 1334: "At the eastern gate there are two enormous idols of brass prostrate on the ground and held by stones, and everyone entering or leaving the mosque treads on them. The site was formerly occupied by an idol temple, and was converted into a mosque on the conquest of the city."*

AJMER: ADHAI-DIN-KA-JHONPRA

With the defeat of Prithviraj Chauhan who ruled from Delhi and Ajmer, the region fell under the Ghorid ruler who, destroyed, looted and then left after placing his loyal slave-general, Qutb-ud-din Aibak on the seat of power. Barring a year's interruption (1194-95), Ajmer remained for the following two centuries under the governors of the sultans of Delhi.

The mosque of Adhai-din-ka-Jhonpra (two-and–a-half-day's hut) took 15 years to build from the destroyed Sanskrit University's carved stones which were further engraved with Islamic calligraphy from the Quran. However, its curious name has given currency to the misconception that the mosque took two-and-a-half days to build. Given the size and scale of the university which existed, it is more likely that this was the time it took to raze it to the ground. The name was given in the late-18th century during Maratha rule, by fakirs who came to commemorate the Urs of Panja Sahib. They used this mosque as a temporary shelter or 'hut' for two-and-a-half days.

The eminent historian Har Bilas Sarda, writing in 1911, had hoped that more excavations would be carried out at the site, since the information found in the six polished, basalt slabs were so useful to reconstruct the missing mosaics of history's jigsaw puzzle.

A ceiling stone (below) of the erstwhile temple-university lies in the open court of the Government Museum in Ajmer, while many others lie deserted within the precincts of Adhai-din-ka-Jhonpra. Of this, novelist and activist Mulk Raj Anand said, "This relief in Ajmer Museum is carved of intricately related figures, obviously intended for decorative effect. It rises above mere adornment by the delicate application of the chisel to achieve a composition which is compact and balanced."

The history of Jahangir's love for the *dargah* at Ajmer began before his birth when his father walked 120 *kos* to ask for a son.

About his visit to the *dargah*, Jahangir writes in ecstatic terms: "When the walls and buildings of the Khwaja's shrine came into view, I went about a kos on foot and assigned my escorts to give money to the poor and needy as they proceeded."

BELOW *A similar example of iconoclasm is the mosque-*madrasa *called Adhai-din-ka-Jhonpra in Ajmer, built on the site of the Sanskrit University by Emperor Vishal Deva. It matched the Raja Bhoj Pathshala of Dhar in its scale which too is now converted into a mosque. On a grand plateau by a scarped hill, beneath the imposing Taragarh Fort, stood the most impressive college, originally a quadrangle of 235 metres x 79 metres, of which only 50 metres remain.*

PAGES 164-165 *In the shadow of Taragarh lies the saint's* dargah, *its dome (right) illuminated by the morning rays.*

LEFT *This cloistered hall made from the material of the destroyed Sanskrit University and a temple to Sarasvati, the goddess of learning, places one pillar above the other for a grander effect.*

ABOVE *A detail of the defaced figures on one of the temple pillars which now form the cloister of the mosque.*

FACING PAGE BOTTOM RIGHT *An intricately-carved stone fragment of the ceiling from the destroyed temple-university.*

BELOW *One of the four slabs of polished basalt excavated in 1875-76. These contain, in finely-inscribed Devanagari script of the12th century, parts of plays in Sanskrit. This is one of two slabs, dated 1153, that record the* Harakeli Nataka *by Vigraharaja in honour of Shiva. Others record the* Lalita Vigraharaja Nataka *by the court poet Somadeva to honour the king of Ajmer of the same name. The last excavations here were done in 1902 when a large, white marble* linga *was found, confirming that this, besides being a university, was also the site of a Hindu, not Jain temple.*

THE AJMER DARGAH

Khwaja Muin-ud-din Chishti of Ajmer established the most influential Sufi Islamic order in India. In no other country had Islam met with a way of life or non-religious dharma – a conduct of righteousness. When it preached the unity of being as man's focus and motive force, it was not new to the Indian ethos.

In India, when Sufism is judged or preached today, many of Hinduism's inherent, benign traits are automatically imputed in the interpretation: non-violence and pacifism, eschewing revenge (without which wars could not have been fought), looking at private property as a negation of faith in God and the refusal to have any relationship with the state (and yet, the *dargah* was built and subsidized by charities of the Mughals and other rulers). Musical recitations, meditation, breath control and periodic confinement for prayer and contemplation were methods that the Sufis are more likely to have learnt in India, rather than taught.

In an elaborately detailed study of the earliest Sufi Chishtiya *silsila* (a chain of transmission) in India, Bruce B Lawrence asks one basic question which would, otherwise be considered blasphemy within the orders of the Faith: "Why did certain Muslims from this part of the world become famous, while others have been forgotten, slighted, or remembered only in relationship to their illustrious contemporaries?" It is his contention that the reputation of a Sufi master largely depended on a biographical process which may be chronologically segmented in two parts: applause noted by contemporaries and that perpetuated by his posthumous fame.

That Ajmer was part of a Hindu kingdom up to the defeat of Prithviraj Chauhan in 1192 added its own flavour to the teaching of Muin-ud-din, the first of the five *shaikhs* of the Chishti order, who died in 1236 in Ajmer. Even though Hindus can be, rather broadly, classified as Shaivite, Vaishnavite and Shakta, as practitioners of a *smarta* religion they have a certain freedom to choose their own deities within a single family worshipping Shiva, Vishnu, or Devi. Hindus can also offer homage even at a Muslim saint's shrine without any compunction, keeping sectarian debates at a lower plane.

Today, Sufism is seen as a benign and syncretic movement between Islam and Hinduism. But the truth could hardly be any farther. However, Sharma's viewpoint has been, "These sufi masters pouring into India from Persia and Central Asia were the products of the post-Hujwirian and post-Ghazalian concordat whereby the esoteric and, according to the consensus of orthodox opinion, rather fanciful flight of unfettered spiritualism was restrained and brought within the four walls of the *sharia* and the *sunna* of the Prophet."

The continued entry of Hindu devotees at a Muslim *dargah* shows the deep-rooted largesse of their religion and their hearts which still remain inclusive of all reverence and all places where prayers are offered with un-divisive thoughts.

FACING PAGE TOP *Shelter is provided to the devout pilgrims who come from far to spend a night in the Garib Nawaz of their saint.*

FACING PAGE BOTTOM *The Nizam Gate built by the rulers of Hyderabad on the main street is the first of three gates of the* dargah.

LEFT *Devotees in the Shahi Masjid built by Emperor Jahangir.*

BELOW *The larger* deg, *or cauldron, presented by Akbar, lies left of the entrance of the* dargah. *For 12 years the emperor visited Ajmer annually to pray for a male heir or because he wanted the* shaikh's *blessings to defeat the invincible Maharana of Mewar.*

PRECEDING PAGES *A view of the resplendent golden city of Swarna Ayodhya showing the palace of Maharaj Nabhiraj, Adinath's father.*

RIGHT *Adinath's mother has a dream in which she sees nine symbols.*

FAR RIGHT & BELOW *A dancer and musicians perform from the rooftop of a mansion to welcome a procession celebrating Adinath's birth.*

BOTTOM CENTRE *The wealthy residents of Ayodhya watch the celestial procession from the rooftop of one of the* havelis.

FACING PAGE TOP LEFT *Seated on the six-trunked elephant Airavata, Indra, the god of rain, arrives with his wife Indrani to take the baby Adinath to Mount Sumeru for a bath.*

FACING PAGE TOP RIGHT *The* apsara *Tilotatama who dances before Adinath, suddenly disappears, reminding him of the transitoriness of all worldly things and inspires his renunciation.*

BOTTOM RIGHT *Adinath, as Rishabhdeva, renounces the world and his clothes at Prayag, attaining salvation after 1,000 years under a banyan tree.*

BELOW *The towering 320 million kilometre high Mount Sumeru surrounded by the circular Jambudvipa island and 13 oceans. Two more of the four Sumeru mountains are shown, these being 270 million kilometres high.*

KISHANGARH: THE REGION OF THE RATHORS

The Maharaja of Jodhpur remains the head of the Rathor clan, but the senior-most of the Ajmer region is the Maharaja of Kishangarh. Understanding this, the British, set up an elaborate hierarchy among the ruling princes and chiefs, gaving the right of a 15-gun salute to Kishangarh. Maharaja Brajraj Singh of Kishangarh, whose father was eliminated in a political murder in independent India, explained: "Even though 17-gun salutes were given only to the head of the clan, Kishangarh's 15-gun salute status was higher than that of the Commander-in-Chief of the Indian army. Besides being the highest among the other 15-gun salute states, it was considered higher than two of the 17-gun salute ones – Tonk and Bharatpur – which they got as heads of their clans."

RIGHT *Brajraj Singh of Kishangarh shows the trophies hunted by his ancestors.*

BELOW *In recent times, Kishangarh's name has been in the forefront for its unique style of miniature painting.*

RIGHT *The 3.5 litre, 1946 Jaguar sports coupe parked in the portico of Manjhela Palace.*

FACING PAGE TOP *The Phool Mahal of Kishangarh, reflected in the waters of its lake.*

FACING PAGE BOTTOM *Kishangarh's horse carriage resembling an early model of a car.*

AJMER UNDER THE BRITISH: RAJPUT ISTIMRARDARS

The vast, sandy plains, serrated by the jugged Aravallis which surround Pushkar and the region of Ajmer-Merwara was ruled from the 7th century CE to the tail-end of the 12th century by the Chauhans, a period of some five clear centuries. And yet, when the British signed *sunnuds*, or agreements, with the ruling chiefs of this area, 15 of the 16 Istimrardars, as they came to be called, were Rathors. The 16th – the Thakur of Sawar – was a Shaktawat from Mewar. This shift of power from one 'fire-born' Rajput clan to another which claimed descent from the 'sun' itself, has as much to do with the initial treachery of the Rathors of Kannauj and the Solankees of Gujarat as it has with the persistence of the Muslim invaders.

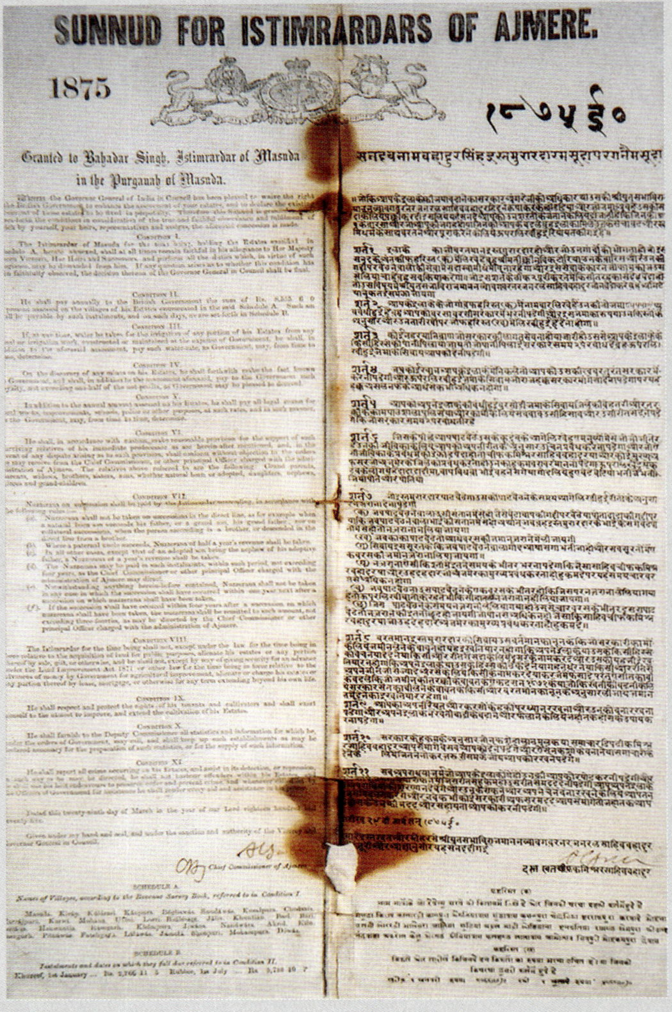
SUNNUD FOR ISTIMRARDARS OF AJMERE.

1875

Granted to Bahadur Singh, Istimrardar of Masuda in the Purganah of Masuda.

The Rathor motto, 'Ranbanka Rathor', itself reveals both their priority and their brand of valour in being the 'battle-crazy Rathors'. However, once the back of the Chauhans had been broken with a combination of insiders' deceit and the outsiders' military might and machinations, a long period of uncertainty followed. The sultan, Muhammad of Ghori held control for a year (1192-93), before the Chauhans reasserted yet again from 1194-95. Then for a spell of two centuries, different Afghan dynasties of Delhi held sway over the area administered by their governors.From 1400 till 1535, the fortunes of Ajmer vacillated between the Ranas of Mewar and the Sultans of Mandu and Gujarat.

The first appearance of the Rathors of Marwar was as late as 1535, lasting only for 21 years. Years of turbulence, mistrust, intrigue and counter-intrigue intervened. In 283 years of history, the Rathors ruled Ajmer for only 39, intermittently sharing power with the Mughals and the Scindias. Running through their history, the traits which weakened them are immediately apparent. Fraternal jealousies most commonly lead to fratricide even patricide if the father did not espouse the cause of his son. When Rao Maldeo died in 1562 in the seventh year of Akbar's reign, according to his wish, his younger son Chandra Sen was made the ruler of Jodhpur. He was backed by a majority of Marwar's nobles which did not strengthen the case of his elder brother Udai Singh who lived in Phalodi. When he heard of Akbar's proposed visit to Nagaur in 1570 he met him and joined his service at Agra. He knew that only if he were backed by the Mughal emperor could he fight his brother. Once Akbar had ascertained his loyalty and bravery, in 1583, Udai Singh, also known as Mota Raja, (the fat king) was put on the Jodhpur throne which incidentally, had been meanwhile given to Raja Rai Singh of Bikaner! This game of royal chequers, patterns all of Rajput history, and yet had not been for this trait of one-upmanship, they would have achieved much greater heights. Mota Raja Udai Singh also offered his daughter, Jagat Gosain Manmati, as a daughter-in-law to Akbar, ensuring his future strength. She was to father the future emperor, Shah Jahan (whose mother was from Jodhpur and grandmother from Amber) making him three-quarters Rajput. The Rathors were only following the example of the Kachhawahas of Amber.

Where mountains could be breached during the planet-making processes and upheavals which had originally pushed the Aravallis to rise up in folds, the people who mixed many bloods and settled here as the Rajputs, knew more than any other, the value of their word. A breach of trust was once considered a sin more fatal than death. While Jahangir had ruefully remarked that he had almost lost his empire for a handfull of millet, it is often forgotten that he had also said, "Even the meanest Rajput has in him a bit of nobility."

ABOVE *Originally, the Istimrardars were 'facilitators' in the revenue collection process and their title originated from the Persian 'intezam', later officialized by the British. The Istimrardars were ruling chiefs, not Rajputana's ruling princes with 19-gun salutes. The text of a* sunnud *signed with the Rao Sahib of Masuda, the largest revenue provider, demarcates their conduct, responsibilities and restrictions. They did not have the powers to condemn anyone to death without consulting the British Resident. By the time the privy purses were discontinued, the Istimrardars had come to be known as 'Ishq Muraries' (gods of love and leisure), confesses one of their descendants!*

FACING PAGE *The viceroy Lord Willingdon poses with the Istimrardars before what is now the Circuit House of Ajmer.*

FOLLOWING PAGES *Bhinai was the seniormost among the Istimrardars. Their albums record their lifestyle.*

The Madalia Fort was the original Bhil Fort at Bhinai.

The raja's palace at Bhinai.

Raja Sardul Singh's coronation.

The bejewelled Kalyan Singh as a groom.

At Raipur, Marwar, the Rathors dine on chowkies *with Maharaja Umaid Singh of Jodhpur at the table.*

The princes' love of hunting started young.

A bull fight in the Bhinai maidan.

Raja Kalyan Singh with his hunted antler.

Royal guests enjoy a round of pig sticking

An exhibition match game of piggy-back polo.

Raja Kalyan Singh of Bhinai arrives as a bridegroom at Sikar, Shekhavati.

The Bhinai raja at a wedding in Palanpur, Gujarat.

Lord Willingdon, the viceroy, with the Indian princes and their sons who studied at Mayo College, Ajmer.

The appealing contrast of the two worlds.

Hospital opening at Bhinai: 'God save the sick' seemed a secondary purpose for the Empire.

A Packard used as a safari car lies sunk in the sand.

PARIKRAMA NOTES & ALBUM

CROSSING THE BARRIER

There are 18 breaches in the long Aravalli ranges through which pilgrims, trading caravans and invading armies have passed. The widest of these openings is between Nand and Khimi, near Pushkar. Thirty kilometres across, this opening would also have been a gateway for the march of the desert, but for the other ranges screening and staggering the constant flow of sand grains which rise and move with every storm.

The north fork of the road to Pushkar winds between the Aravalli ranges and reaches Burha Pushkar, the first of the three Pushkars, near Kanas village. En route, it passes the villages of Makarvali and Hokra with Makrol Mata between them to the right and later Badar Mata. The pilgrimage point of Shuddha Vapi is on the left, beyond Burha Pushkar. The road then leads to Madhya Pushkar on a short, dusty track to the right, then back to the Neem-Pipal Avenue, with the *parikrama* centres of Bhat Baye/Ganesh Kund and finally to the toll post at the entry to Pushkar.

The south fork of the road, snaking over a defile in the Nagpahar (literally, serpent mountain, but named after the Gurjara king, Nagabhata I), coils and straightens past Leela Sevri village where the mountainous part of the pilgrimage of one of the three sacred *parikramas* of Pushkar can begin (see pp. 58-67 for details of the three *parikramas*).

VARAHA TEMPLE 1

The largest ancient temple at the lakeside pilgrimage of Pushkar is that of Varaha, the boar incarnation of Vishnu. Two of the forms which earlier legends ascribe to Brahma – a

tortoise (Kurma) and a boar (Varaha) – are in later works, ascribed to the second and third avatars of Vishnu. This may well explain the presence of a large Varaha Temple at Pushkar. Legend has it that Varaha rescued the earth from the depths of the primeval waters, where it had been dragged down by a demon. The presence of this deity at Pushkar may be associated with Vedic literature in which Prajapati (who finally merged with the creative aspect of Brahma) raised the earth-goddess from the primeval waters as Emusha, the black boar incarnation of Vishnu.

This temple was first destroyed by the Ghaznavid army in the reign of Arnaraja (1123-50) and later by Aurangzeb. Colonel Broughton wrote in 1810 in his *Letters from the Marhatta Camp:* "The temple of Varahji, as it now stands, presents only the small remains of the ancient temple which was overthrown by the bigoted zeal of Aurangzeb, and is said to have been 150 feet [46 metres] in height and covered with the finest specimens of Hindu sculpture."

A heavy, 10-foot spear of Hada Chhatrasal of Bundi now lies by the Varaha idol, a reminder of the Rajput saviours and restorers of this temple.

Even today, three centuries after the last desecration and destruction, broken stone lintels, carvings and architectural titbits can be seen strewn all around Pushkar. The Varaha Ghat remains one of the important ghats and the 7.5 *kos parikrama* normally begins from here.

The boar personifies the sacrifice; his feet being the Vedas; his tusk the sacrificial posts to which the victim is tied; his teeth, the sacrificial offerings; his mouth, the altar; his tongue, the fire; his hair, the sacrificial grass; his eyes, day and night; his head, the place of Brahma; his name, the hymns of the Vedas; his nostrils, all the oblations; his snout, the ladle of oblation; his voice, the chanting of the Sama Veda; his body, the hall of sacrifice; his joints, the different ceremonies; and his ears containing the properties of voluntary and obligatory rites.

Entering through the gateway to the Varaha and Kurmanchal Ghats, one also sees the home of Rani Ahilya Bai Holkar of Indore, who was a great Shaivite devotee reputed to have built 144 temples to Shiva.

NEELKANTH MAHADEV TEMPLE 2

An ancient but simple temple in a walled court, this sanctuary gives the semblance of a family shrine. The *linga* is a local, unchiselled boulder, suggesting a *svayambhu*, or self-appeared one. The floor is paved in marble tiles and the old *yoni-patta* now lies practically buried.

ATMATESHVAR MAHADEV TEMPLE 3

See p. 38

GUPTESHVAR MAHADEV TEMPLE 4

There was another Shiva temple in the original *parikrama* lists, called

Gupteshvar Mahadev, the 'hidden' Shiva, which now seems to live up to its name; no one today is able to identify it. It has been suggested that this *linga* may now be submerged in the lake. This is not unlikely, as Rousselet records in 1878, "There was such an insatiable demand for this sacred ground that the architects appear to have taken advantage of some extraordinary season to advance into the very bed of the lake. The successive risings of the water, which has regained and even overflowed the original brooks, have immersed a considerable number of these monuments, of which nothing can now be seen but the domes...."

During the search for this 'hidden' temple, an amusing signage

JAHANGIR & HIS PALACE AT PUSHKAR

Jahangir records in his memoirs, *Tuzuk-i-Jahangiri*, his iconoclasm at the Varaha Temple:

> *On the seventh of Azar [November 18], I went out to tour and hunt at Pushkar Tank, one of the Hindus' major holy places. They say things about its virtues that no sound mind would accept. It is located three kos from Ajmer. I set out for there and hunted water fowl at the tank for two or three days. Then I returned to Ajmer. All around the edges of the tank can be seen ancient and new temples, which the Hindus call dewhra. Rana Shankar, the uncle of the Rana and a great amir in our state, built one of them so elaborately that it is said he spent a lac of rupees on it. I went to see it. There I saw something made of carved black stone. From the neck up it had the shape of a pig's head, while the rest resembled a man's body. It is the Hindus' vain belief that once upon a time for some reason known only to the Omniscient, he appeared in this form. They therefore revere and worship this form. I ordered the hideous thing smashed and thrown into the tank.*
>
> *After inspecting the building, I saw on the summit of the mountain a white dome, to which people flock from all directions. I asked what it was. They said there was a yogi there, and simpletons who go to see him are given a handful of flour. They put it in their mouths and make the sound of animals they have injured sometimes, so that by means of that act they can wash away the sin. I ordered this place destroyed, the yogi driven away, and the idol that was in the dome smashed.*

ABOVE *An itinerant ascetic from Bengal takes refuge in what was once the palace of the Mughal emperor, Jahangir. He reads, lost in his thoughts, beyond the meaning of life and possessions, unaware that an inscription above the doorway in the adjoining palace had once optimistically wished otherwise: "The King Nur-ud-din Jahangir, son of King Akbar: may he remain happy on the throne while the world lasts.... Many welcome victories come to him from the unknown at all times. By his order this auspicious palace in Pushkar was completed; may the foundation of the palace of his grandeur be as high as the sky. I asked for its chronogram and a voice came from the unknown: May this palace of Jahangir in Pushkar always remain inhabited."*

Jahangir was the son of Akbar from his Rajput wife Jodha Bai of Amber (later Jaipur). She was not forced to convert to Islam and maintained her own palace at Fatehpur Sikri where she was allowed to worship her idols in her temple. Such ignorance and intolerance from her son is surprising. Two other factors may have played a part in Jahangir's iconoclasm. For one, it is anathema for a Muslim to eat the meat of a wild boar, leave aside consider the animal fit for worship. He does mention in his memoirs hunting boar and sending the pork to his Christian friends. The second factor was the Mughals' avowed enmity with the Ranas of Mewar/Udaipur.

The inscription on his Pushkar palace mentions with some pride that he "conquered the territory of the Rana [of Chittor] in the tenth year of his accession to the throne [1615 CE]".

The fact that the Varaha Temple was repaired by Sagar, the brother of Rana Pratap, in Akbar's time, may well have made it a symbol of contention. It would, however, be too much to expect Jahangir to recognize in the boar incarnation the inherent, evolutionary wisdom of the *dashavatara*s of Vishnu. These coincide with Darwin's evolution of man: from a water creature to an amphibian, before he walked the earth. Varaha is the third incarnation of Vishnu with a special role in the recurring myth of the earth being rescued from the waters.

DR CR FRANCIS AT PUSHKAR (1848)

Officers of the East India Company and the Christian missionaries too had their own opinions about the Hindu pilgrims and their pilgrimage. Dr Charles Richard Francis, MB of the Bengal Medical Establishment was the first European to record Rajasthan in his drawings, published in London in 1848. After drawing "a Hindoo family, wending its way to one of the holiest, and most celebrated, spots acknowledged by the religion of the Brahmin," he writes, "And thus have they jogged on for many a mile. Now the object of their journey is near at hand: and sad indeed is it to reflect, that this little family has ventured to encounter all the difficulties attendant upon a long pilgrimage, solely with the hope of becoming more highly esteemed by the senseless idols of their faith. Were the Hindoos' zeal, now alas! devoted to the cause of idolatry, engaged with the same fervour in that of Christianity, how great a lesson of unwearied patience would be taught many of the professing followers of our Saviour's Gospel."

He also adds, "Poshkur is one of the strong-holds of Hindooism; there the sad infatuation rages with great force. At certain seasons of the day may be heard the sound of the going, loudly proclaiming the devotional spirit of those who are performing upon it. By the door of a temple, or at the corner of a street, groups assemble for prayer; thus calling in mind the words of our Saviour: 'And when thou prayest, thou shalt not be as the hypocrites are: for they love to pray standing in the synagogues, and in the corners of the street that they may be seen of men'. Painting another marvellous view of Pushkar, he concludes "Be our's the pleasing task to unfold to that 'untutored mind' the Source from whence all goodness flows; and to turn it from the shrine of idolatry to the worship of the living God!"

BELOW *A mid-19th-century lithograph drawn on stone by JC Anderson, shows a Hindu family en route to Pushkar, before the invincible Taragarh fort of Ajmer situated high on the hilltop.*

near the Pushkar *thana*, or police station, appeared as Thaneshvar Mahadev.

BHUTESHVAR MAHADEV TEMPLE **5**

Between the large Varaha Temple and the discreet Neelkanth Mahadev lies the site of Bhuteshvar Mahadev, with an old *linga* set on a relatively new marble base.

A circumambulation can only be made from outside the small family-sized temple, and the space for rituals is limited.

BIHARI-JI/BAI-JI TEMPLE **6**

Adjoining the palace of Man Singh I of Jaipur, lies a large and impressive temple built by the *rani* of Sawai Jagat Singh (r. 1803-18). The lascivious Jagat Singh spent all his time with 20 other queens and 24 official concubines, and perhaps his *rani's* only option was to take recourse to religion. History records that he died heirless, probably murdered in the harem after having signed the Treaty of Defensive Alliance with the British in 1818. At one point, he entrusted half his kingdom to Ras Kapur, a courtesan whose music and beauty had enamoured him.

This is a temple of the Vallabhacharya sect, founded by a Telugu Brahman child prodigy in south India, which has a large following among the business and trading communities of most of western India. They propagate a joyous worship offering their god Krishna all the luxuries which they enjoy. Eight daily rituals of waking, bathing and dressing, feeding betel leaves, being taken out to graze cattle, returning home, being entertained with dance and music, and finally being put to sleep, are all conducted with full ceremony. Currently, the Gauda priest living in this temple at Pushkar treats the temple as his residence. Visitors are required to seek permission to have the gate unlocked, and are generally made to feel rather unwelcome.

The gurus are called Maharajas. Vallabha's son, Vitthalnath had eight sons whose disciples are the Goswamis of Nathadwara today. Pampered by excesses, they even offered their devotees the water with which they washed their feet or rinsed their mouth, records Walker. In 1862, a case of licentiousness in the Bombay High Court brought the cult to notoriety, but it has since been reformed.

There is, curiously, no seat of the Madhavacharis at Pushkar, the fourth Vaishnava sect formed in the 13th century by a Kannarese Brahman of Udipi. He countered Shankaracharya's monism with his

own dualism. "How can the human soul unite with Brahma after death when it is separate during life?" he had queried and endlessly debated.

Together, the four Vaishnava sects set out to counter the four Shaivite *peeths* that the reformer, Adi Shankaracharya had set up at Shringeri, Puri, Dwarka and Badrinath.

UTTARAMUKHI BALAJI **7**

To cite the Mahabharata: "On Pushkardvipa there is a Nyagrodha tree which is Brahma's highest abode. In that Brahma dwells, worshipped by gods and demons." The ecological importance of trees, even for the illiterate, was brought out by underlining such beliefs. Today, many large *barh* trees exist at Pushkar and this one is walled away from the

Saptarishi Ghat with an iron gate. When open, it leads to a café whose claim to fame is the presence of psychedelic bulbs and tube lights which flash in it after dark.

CHATURNATH/BAVAN BHAIRON TEMPLE **8**

This modest temple of Bavan Bhairon or 52 Bhairons is located off the southern end of the Pushkar lake and forms part of the *parikrama*. Since Bhairon is a field spirit, it is usually worshipped on the village outskirts, also related with the cult of dogs who guard notional boundaries. Worshipped mainly on Sundays, this temple represented by natural *linga*-like stones painted in saffron or pasted with tinsel paper, offers the choice of worshipping a

different Bhairon on each of the 52 Sundays of the year.

It is this figure of 52 which has come to be accepted as auspicious, and has given Pushkar its Bavan (52) Ghat myth. Beginning in the 9th century CE with just 12 ghats, it is only now that a count can be stretched to 52 ghats.

BRAHMA TEMPLE **9**

Towering above the Pushkar skyline, the *shikhar* of the Brahma Temple shows the many pinnacled, smaller *'shikhars'* which compose its form. The word *shikhar* literally means a peak, and is used in temple architecture to represent the superstructure which rises over the *garbha-griha*, or 'womb-home' which is the sanctum sanctorum. This temple was destroyed by Aurangzeb, and a period of fear and confusion followed. It was first repaired in 1719 by a Brahman devotee, a woman from Jaipur named Phundi Bai, "the daughter of Girdhar Das and mother of Shambhu Ram". It was then rebuilt by Maharaja Sawai Jai Singh II of Jaipur in 1727. In 1809, Gokul Chand Parekh, a minister of the Scindias, repaired it for Rs 130,000.

The marble statue of Surya standing attendant at the Brahma Temple is shown in boots. It is pointed out that while all the gods are shown with bare feet, the figure of Surya wears an ancient warrior's boots. This was considered a luxury accorded to him by the iconographers who did not want his feet to be scorched by the heat generated by him!

KAPALESHVAR MAHADEV TEMPLE **10**

This ancient temple, accessed by a few steps, supposedly marks the raised site near Brahma's *yajna* from where Shiva threw the *kapala*, or skull, and disrupted the rituals (see p. 38 for the legend). It was founded by the Naga sadhu Pitheshvar with 50 acres of land. This has become a constantly contested property; in order to acquire its *siddha* seat, there has been much quarrelling and

litigation. Recently a murder was committed, and its management was put under a trust.

KALIKA MATA TEMPLE 11 17

Half a kilometre above the Marwar bus stand lies this ancient Kali temple, approached through a large,

fortified gateway. Its origin is related to a tale of a fight with demons. The goddess' *saptadhatu* idol is believed to be very powerful and is currently worshiped by Pandit Hira Lal Sarbaria.

PAPMOCHINI TEMPLE 12 18

On the northern peak sits the temple of Papmochini (sin-absolving), housing Ekadashi Mata. This is considered the best place to seek retribution for killing any

living being. It is believed that Ashvathama, cursed by Krishna in the Mahabharata to roam the world for three thousand years, comes here annually to seek retribution. He had unwittingly killed the unborn baby of Uttara with the *brahmashirastra*, a powerful missile given to him by his father Dronacharya. The devout undertake their climb to the Papmochini Temple in the west with a spirit of stoic humility, equating effort and sacrifice with spiritual reward. Worship in this temple is currently carried out by Pandit Vishnu Mishra, a Parashara priest. A panoramic view from the Papmochini Temple shows the lake on the left and the sandy *mela* grounds on the right, which lead on to the vast desert plains of Marwar. According to legend, the Gurjara girl, Gayatri atoned for her husband Brahma's sin of marrying her instead of waiting for his wife Savitri to arrive at the *yajna*. The temple derives its name from this legend, and is also called Gayatri Peeth, where retribution for sins is easily granted.

HANUMAN BAORI 13 19

This small, but most innovative and impressive *baori* near a Hanuman temple (which has two sanctums) lies by the Marwar Bus Stand in a greatly neglected state. While spiral steps descend to the water, a three-arched *tibari,* shaded by trees, provides a cool spot for pilgrims to

catch the breeze. The courtyard of the temple is very charming, and still has the feel of an ancient structure. Unfortunately, the well is dry and clogged, and the wall by the temple entrance has become a place for public conveniences.

BHAT BAYE /GANESH KUND 14 16

Nagabhata, the most renowned Gurjara king of the area, is reputed to have had 900,000 cows. As they grazed every day, he would supervise the building of this and other stepwells. The Bhat Baye (possibly derived from his name) also takes another derivative form of the Bhatrai Mata, a temple built within a stepwell at the toll entry post of Pushkar. The stepwells of Bagravat Baye, below the Savitri Temple, is also believed to have been built by him.

By the Bhat Baye *baori*, a more recently established Ganesh Temple has become very popular. Since it lies 2 kilometres before the entrance to Pushkar, it is convenient to first worship there before embarking on the pilgrimage. This site also has a role in marital rites: the first wedding invitation is given here, and on the first Wednesday after the marriage, *prasad* from here is offered to all relatives. Consequently, the younger generation calls this the Ganesh Baori or Ganesh Kund.

MADHYA PUSHKAR *See p. 43*

SHUDDHA VAPI/GAYA KUND *See p. 59*

JYESHTHA/BURHA PUSHKAR *See p. 42*

LAL BIHARI RADHA MADHAV TEMPLE 18 1 22

The temple of Lal Bihari Radha Madhav in Leela Sevri village lies at the foot of the hill, about 2 kilometres short of Pushkar on the south fork. Many pilgrims begin their sacred journey from this tough, mountainous part. The temple was rebuilt by Sant Doodhadhari, and its black stone idols – with Radha in a lighter stone – are considered to be from

the original temple. Pandit Vishal Anand conducts daily worship here. A large masonry throne for the deity or the priest recalls the scale of activities which once took place here. An annual mela is held on *Bhadon Sudi Ashtami*.

KAPILESHVAR MAHADEV/KAPIL MUNI ASHRAM 19

A deep and ancient stepwell, just by the main road to Pushkar, marks the spot which is reputed to be the ashram of Kapila Muni, a great but fierce sage. Although the name Kapila is used as a synonym both for Shiva and Vishnu in the Anushasana Parva of the Mahabharata, the sage was a devotee of Shiva, and this is why a Shiva temple exists at his ashram. He was a great authority on the

Sankhya philosophy and the Vedas, and wrote the Sankhyapravachana and the Tattvasamasa.

PANDESHVAR MAHADEV TEMPLE 20 2

Like many pilgrim sites in India, at Pushkar too, it is believed that the five Pandavas arrived here and worshipped a small *shivalinga* above the village of Leela Sevri. Accessed by a circuitous route overgrown with thorny scrub, this small temple is hardly visited today.

north Indian centre – besides Vrindavan – lies at Salemabad, near Kishangarh. (It is said that Akbar was camping here when news of his son Salim's birth at Ajmer was received, thus the name Salemabad.) Nimbarka was a Telugu Brahman who earned his name because he arrested the sunset by hanging its last ray *(arka)* on a *nimba* tree so that his ascetic-guest could cook and eat before the sunset.

Nimbarka's 'dualistic non-dualism', in which both finite man and nature depend on Brahma but are independent of him, emphasized *bhakti* (devotion) over meditation. The Nimbandis emphasize the worship of Radha along with Krishna.

Parashurama Devacharya was sent from Vrindavan to set up his *dhuni* (sacred fire) at Salemabad to protect the Hindus who came to worship from Merta and were attacked by Yavana *tantrikas*. He bathed daily at Pushkar and was much feared in the region. He blessed Sher Shah Suri with a son and was given a *tamra-patra* (copper-plate inscription). However, valuable literature of this sect was destroyed in Aurangzeb's time

YAJNA GHAT 34

This ghat marks the actual site of the fire rite. Paved with a chequered floor of black and white marble, it now forms one of the prominent ghats of Pushkar. Yet, nothing particularly distinguishes this ghat from the others except an old and harmonious idol of Ganesha, flanked by his wives Riddhi and Siddhi – the means and the end.

Brahma is believed to have bathed here after completing the *yajna*. The Shiva temple here was made by one Jaguji from the *darbar* of Jodhpur.

BADRI NARAYAN TEMPLE 35

This domed, fortified temple is one among the oldest of Pushkar's temples to Vishnu. Situated on a hill among the back alleys not far from the Brahma Temple, it has gradually lost its importance with modern-day worshippers.

RANGANATH VENUGOPAL/ OLD RANG-JI TEMPLE 36

This temple, built in 1844 by Seth Puranmal Ganeriwal of Lakshmangarh, Shekhavati, is the first temple of the Ramanuja sect in Rajasthan. Commonly known as the Old Rang-ji Temple, its chief deity is a flute-playing Krishna as Ranganath Venugopal.

The Ganeriwals hail from Ganeri village which lies between Sikar and Sujangarh. But their ancestral *haveli*, the grandest in Shekhavati, was built with four large courtyards in Lakshmangarh and is well known as the Char Chowk Haveli. The inspiration to build this temple came from Anantachari Maharaj of Kanchipuram, whose statue is installed within. Since its inception, Dravida Brahmans have performed all rituals according to the Pancharata Vidhi, complete with a procession of the *vahanas,* or vehicles, of the gods shaded with gilt-embroidered umbrellas.

Built in the traditional style, the temple has no *shikhar* like the north Indian temples, but a *gopuram* over the entrance gateway. The architecture uses the lime and mortar technique of Shekhavati, including mythological frescos in the Italian fresco-*buono* technique and figures in relief. The temple boasts of the largest monolithic statue of a four-armed Krishna in black Kadappa stone from Tamil Nadu. It is difficult to conceive how such a large idol was transported all the way. As early as 1864, this traditional temple

showed its progressiveness by allowing foreigners in the outer *parikrama* and a marble plaque records this event.

Besides the statue of Venugopal, there are others: Ranganath of Srirangam lying on a *panchmukhi* or five-headed Sheshanaga; Shri Ramanujacharya and the 11 Alvars; the goddesses Lakshmi and

ABOVE *The main deity of the temple is the four-armed Venugopala, of which two play the flute. He is flanked by Rukmani and Satyabhama. The three, smaller black stone idols are made of* panchadhatu *metal.*

Godamma Godamba who flank the *parikrama* of the main platform.

There are already two imposing temples of the Ramanuja sect in Kanishtha Pushkar – the old and the new Ranganatha – and a third one is being built at Jyeshtha or Burha Pushkar.

GAU GHAT 37

Well located towards the middle of the market street, Gau Ghat's importance in the *parikrama* is evident from its broad landing and wide steps. The importance of the cow, after whom the ghat is named, need hardly be emphasized for the

LEFT *Avatara Charitra, written in 1676 by Barhath Naraharidas at Pushkar, which lies at Bhakti Dham of the Charans in Ajmer, is the only known publication on the 24 avatars of Vishnu. This most certainly inspired the Ganeriwals of Lakshmangarh, who built a Vaishnav temple of the south Indian Ramanuja sect at Pushkar, to carve more than the customary 10 Vishnu avatars on the lintels of their temple's inner sanctum. Naraharidas' 24 avatars make an interesting list: (The* dashavataras *are marked in asterisks): 1. Adi Varaha*, 2. Sankadi, 3. Yagna, 4. Nara-Narayana, 5. Kapila, 6. Dattatreya, 7. Rishabha, 8. Dhruva, 9. Prithu, 10. Hayagriva, 11. Kurma*, 12. Matsya*, 13. Narasimha*, 14. Vamana*, 15. Hari, 16. Hansa, 17. Manvantara, 18. Dhanavantari, 19. Parasurama*, 20. Ved Vyasa, 21. Shri Rama*, 22. Shri Krishna*, 23. Buddha*, 24. Kalki*.*

Hindus, particularly at places of pilgrimage. The temple has a particular significance because it was built after the Rajputs of this area requested the Mughal governor to respect their cows as they needed protection and veneration.

A large, white marble cenotaph commemorating the Maratha general Sant-ji, as well as a temple of Kalyan-ji, stand by the ghat. The temple of Kalyan-ji was shifted here from Indra Ghat in recognition of the importance of Gau Ghat.

It is on Gau Ghat that the ashes of Jawaharlal Nehru, Lal Bahadur Shastri, Jay Prakash Narayan, Indira Gandhi, Rajiv Gandhi and other national dignitaries were immersed. The Sikh Guru Gobind Singh also held a recitation of the Guru Granth Sahib here in 1705.

GURU GOBIND SINGH GHAT

Although the Gobind Ghat stone plaque is on Gau Ghat, the municipality has now accorded this name to the ghat near the Man Ghat of Jaipur where a large *gurudwara* has risen in the vicinity. Since *Kartik Purnima* coincides with

Guru Nanak's birthday and the Guru is reported to have visited Pushkar on that day, the Sikhs also consider a bath in its waters, auspicious.

Guru Gobind Singh, the 10th Sikh guru, visited Pushkar in 1705. His *hukamnamah*, or command, written out on a parchment scrap still lies with the Punjabi Pandas Lal Singh-Madan Singh Dariwala, near the Gau Ghat (below).

QUEEN MARY GHAT

Queen Mary visited India only once for the 1911 coronation *darbar* – when she visted Mayo College in Ajmer and supposedly the ghats of

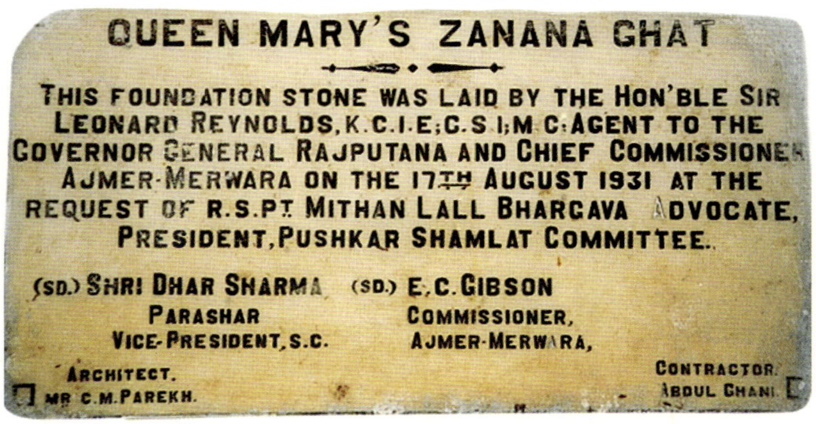

Pushkar too. Curiously, this marble plaque was only put in 1931 and the ladies' bathing ghat is named after her. The date is not connected to the coronation of George V which was in 1910, or with his death in 1936, or her death which was in 1953.

REHGARAN GHAT (MAHATMA GANDHI GHAT)

Families of monkeys innocently perch above an important plaque whose letters have been erased with time. It was here, at the Rehgaran Ghat, that the ashes of Mahatma Gandhi, the father of the independent Indian nation, were immersed after he was assassinated. The ghat is now also named after him since it was here that the lowest among the lower castes – the *rehgars*, or leather workers – bathed. Gandhi had worked for the upliftment of the 'untouchables', or *achhut*, renaming them as the Harijans, or people of god.

RAM-LAKSHMAN TEMPLE 38

Supposedly an old temple, this was renovated by the Poddars, a wealthy Marwari trading family, and is now reached by a steep flight of broad stairs which lead to a courtyard. The idols of Rama, Lakshmana, Bharata, Shatrughana and Janaki – are housed here. These are currently worshipped by Kishan Lal Pujari.

ADHAR SHILA 8

High above the ashram of Vishvamitra and 3 kilometres from Lakshmi Pol, a gigantic boulder balances precariously over a tiny stone estimated to weigh only 3 kilograms. It is an arduous two-hour climb, but the view of Pushkar – and of Ajmer and beyond – more than compensate for the effort. It is naively believed by some that each year on the festival of Deepavali this rock turns to gold for a few seconds!

SANKATAMOCHAN BARH GANESH TEMPLE 11

The Sankatamochan Barh Ganesh Temple lies at the foot of the Savitri Temple, acting as a base camp for pilgrims. They catch their breath in the shade of a banyan or Nyagrodha tree, believed to take away one's troubles. This site first became a pilgrim stop when Ram Kishan Nagori of Pushkar made a thirst-quenching *piao* here. Later, his wife built a temple dedicated to Santoshi Ma. Following this, on the trunk of the banyan tree, a vegetal

image of Ganesha miraculously appeared. The roots which hang from the main banyan have sprouted independent roots over the years, and devotees suspend these racines with dry coconut offerings, giving it double *vanaspati shakti*, or vegetal power. The term, *"Shri Ganesha Karna"* (to begin work auspiciously) applies here as an invocation for the ascent to the Savitri Temple.

SAVITRI TEMPLE 12

Pushkar has craggy, dry hills on three sides, two capped by temples which seem like little forts. Ratnagiri, the highest hill on the south-west, houses the goddess Savitri, the estranged wife of Brahma. The slopes of these hills harvest the rain waters and fill the lake Sarovar. To the north is the temple of Papmochini, whereas in the eastern hills lie many of the caves and ashrams of the sages. The strenuous pilgrimage to the Savitri Temple, 2 kilometres each – first by road and then by foot – wins merit and spiritual reward for the devout. The harder one tries, the more *tapas* (heat generated by penance) is gained.

Although Brahma's first wife was annoyed that he had taken on another wife who performed the *yajna* which initiated the pilgrimage of Pushkar (making her curse him never to be worshipped by anyone), later the two wives made peace and even united to ask for boons for their husband. They agreed that in the future, Savitri would always be worshipped before Gayatri. Even today, the first *arti* is performed at the Savitri Temple, and, only when the conch is sounded, do the prayers at the Gayatri Temple begin. Women devotees offer camphor for the longevity of their husbands.

The idols of both Savitri and Gayatri are now installed at the Savitri Temple. Though the idol of Savitri supposedly dates back to the 7th century CE, the temple itself was built by the Bangar family in the early 20th century.

NANDA-PRACHI-SARASVATI SANGAM 13 3

Where the three rivers Nanda-Prachi-Sarasvati merge and mingle their waters (see p. 36 for the legend), a beautiful ancient temple stands. It is known as Govaliya Gokul or the Old Gokul, an obvious recreation of the original pilgrimage by the same name in Braj, the land of Krishna. This is

one among the many efforts to locate all mythology at Pushkar, and make it into a composite pilgrimage. The priest Damodar Das enlightens visitors about the large-scale *mela* held here each year on *Janamashtami*, the birth date of Krishna.

NANDRAI MATA 14 4

Beyond the south-western periphery of Pushkar, where Shiva protects it from any evil effects, lies the village of Nand. High on a pinnacled hill above the village is the temple of Nandrai Mata where villagers climb steep steps to offer coconuts to the goddess. Spectacular views including the *triveni* Sangam await the devout, and admiring such a vast and wondrous countryside from where god himself surveys his planet, can only be therapeutic.

It was here that patriots/publishers from the area climbed and raised their cry to rid India of all traitors.

KAKRESHVAR-MAKRESHVAR TEMPLES 15 2

A curious tale is often told at Pushkar, particularly where temples lie destroyed. Besides the version that these temples were looted and destroyed by Mahmud of Ghazni and his armies, there is another recurring tale which seems bred on Hindu-Jain rivalry. A Jain saint meditated at Pushkar for several years and was served by a simple and devout disciple. Every day he would cut firewood and carry it on his head from the forest to Pushkar. He would then cook the food and serve the saint who never once compensated him. Despite this, the disheartened disciple continued to serve the Jain saint, till he lost his hair with the rubbing of the wood that he carried daily on his head. When people noticed this and

began to chide him, the frustrated disciple cursed the saint from his heart and there was a great rain of sand grains and the Jain temples began to crumble and fall!

In all the oral narrations of this improbable tale, the 'rain of sand' is common, perhaps recalling a historic incident when the temples were actually physically destroyed and a lot of rubble and dry mortar must have fallen. In subsequent years, the migrating sand dunes covered the unattended temples. In 2003, in the course of digging the foundations for a house, some Jain statues were unearthed at Pushkar, and these too are now housed in the Government Museum, Ajmer. At Makreshvar Temple, which once stood by the Sarasvati (now a subterranean rivulet), there is a rare standing idol of Gajanana. About 1 kilometre from Makreshvar lies the Kakreshvar Temple which is some 2.5 kilometres from Kanbaye. Following the vogue for things modern, a white Rama temple on a nearby hill seems to have become the focus of attention for about a decade.

KANBAYE 16 1

The Puranic pilgrimage route of Pushkar ordains that the 84 *kos parikrama* should begin and end here. However, today, despite the motorable road, Kanbaye is not often visited by pilgrims. Behind the modest temple which stands among cultivated fields, sits the Surya Kund, a low-lying area which fills up with water only in the monsoons. This is likened to the

Ksheer Sagar of the Vishnu Purana where Sheshanaga provided a bed for Vishnu. A large, black stone idol of this theme was the original deity of Kanbaye, later replaced by Krishna-Radha. It was in the Surya Kund of Kanbaye that Chyavan Rishi, who meditated on the Rohit mountain nearby, bathed and was transformed into a young man. His final resting place on the Dhaunsi Pahar is near Narnaul in Haryana and merits a visit.

VAIDYANATH MAHADEV TEMPLE 24 9

Ten kilometres north-east of Pushkar lies the ancient site of one of the four important *shivalingas* guarding the four directions. By legend it seems to be a re-creation of one of the 12 *jyotirlingas*, the one at the Vaidyanath Dham near Patna in Bihar, where Ravana worshipped Shiva and was granted the boon of immortality.

Vaidyanath is reached by a metalled road which stops by large banyan trees, creating the atmosphere of a Vedic *vatika* (forest). Five stepped reservoirs, which overflow from one into the other, create an idyllic atmosphere where pilgrims have a series of *dharamshalas* to cook in and picnic. The late Sant Vishnu Maharaj greatly improved the provision for utensils and firewood – a tradition maintained by his disciple Brahmachari Maharaj. An annual *mela* is held here on *Bhadav Sudi Gyaras.*

MAKROL MATA/MARKANDEY ASHRAM 25 10

North-east of Pushkar, around 2.5 kilometres from Baidyanath, lies the Markandey Ashram where Makrol Mata is worshipped below large trees whose exposed roots cling to the rocks. Large, calcified rocks by a trickling stream are rubbed to get the *bhashma*, or ashes, held sacred for Shiva. Rawat priests maintain this ashram.

There is an age-old legend of the young sage Markandeya who was destined to die at 16. But his ardent devotion to Shiva brought his life's end to a dramatic moment whereby Shiva himself manifested from his symbol of veneration, the *linga*. With fiery eyes he waved his terrifying trident and battleaxe and beat the drum of creation to scare away someone no less than Yama, the lord of death. Yama is usually represented in the Markandeya legend with his hands folded and raised, acknowledging the superiority of Shiva. His *kalapasa*, the noose of time with which he ensnares his victims, lies snapped beneath his mount, the buffalo, in a rendering by Ravi Varma. Shiva, the lord who ends destruction, has thus shown to his devotees that even death could be 'destroyed' if he so willed, and the logic has prevailed.

LOMASH RISHI/ROJARI MATA 26 11

The sage Lomasha was renowned as a storyteller. As a narrator of Puranic episodes, he was a celebrated pupil of Vyasa, the compiler of the Mahabharata. He was also called Suta, a generic term for bards and chroniclers. The

picturesque Lomasha Rishi Ashram near Pushkar, may be related to the presence of the prominent Varaha Temple. In the Mahabharata, it was Lomasha Rishi who told Dharmaputra the story of the demon Narakasura and the incarnation of Vishnu as Varaha. There is another legend in which Lomasha advises the gods to make weapons out of the bones of the sage Dadhichi, in whose name a ghat exists at Pushkar.

The idol of Rojari Mata is worshipped in the temple of this ashram.

SHIVA TEMPLE, THANVLA 5

In 956 CE, this impressive Shiva temple was raised above a *linga*, 9 kilometres north-west from Pushkar. Built according to classical norms within a protective court-wall, the *shikhar* of the temple is now heavily shaded with trees. High stone berths in the domed entrance have markings of sandal grinding and blade sharpenings, perhaps for animal sacrifices. The statues on the outer *parikrama* have been badly defaced by armies that passed this way.

BHAIRAV NATH, THANVLA 6

Off the village of Thanvla, under an old banyan tree, lies an ancient Bhairav shrine. Stones daubed with tinsel and bits of old carved stone effigies are offered oblations which include alcohol. Gorakhnathis live and worship here, lighting little clay lamps, hoping that someday soon their work of raising an impressive temple to Bhairav will materialize.

BADA ASAN 7

Bada Asan near Thanvla is where Raja Bhartrihari renounced the world and did penance. He made four balls from the *vibhuti* (ashes) of his *dhuni* and gave them to four disciples who took them to Jodhpur

(Siddhyanath), Mewada (near Padu), Didwana and Bada Asan in Rajasthan.

The *samadhis* of the various Gorakhnathi heads at Bada Asan can be seen in the courtyards and rooms, showing the antiquity of the site.

GHATI KE HANUMAN TEMPLE 23

While driving from Ajmer, this Hanuman temple is situated before

the defile in the Nagpahar which leads to Pushkar. Earlier, most pilgrims, exhausted by the climb, used to pause here for a drink and rest. Today, many prefer to take a bus or a jeep. The large stone idol of Ghati ke Hanuman, who presides over the 'gorge', shows him crushing the demon Rahu, who is part of Brahma's court. Painted in saffron and pasted with silver leaf foil, its looming presence shines in the dark.

Crossing over into the Pushkar valley, pilgrims can only be delighted by its vast open view and a small temple to Kalki, the 10th avatar of Vishnu prophesied to appear in the future in Orissa.

BHANVTA DEVI TEMPLE 24

Over 40 kilometres from Pushkar, this ancient temple of Bhanvta Devi dates back to over a millennium. It has many popular legends associated with it. Over the years, it became partly buried in the shifting sand dunes and the hollow space beneath its *shikhar* became a hideout for

Robin Hood-style bandits. Climbing on its roof, one can still see how a large stone slab can be moved to block a whole room where several people can crouch and hide. The powerful goddess below is a great favourite of the Rajputs who venerate her with bottles of alcohol. According to oral tradition, she accepts only one peg, not a second, and should she refuse, this is taken as a bad omen.

Unfortunately, a well-meaning businessman has tried to restore it by excavating the sand and adding a modern verandah with cement pillars and mosaic floors. This has significantly destroyed its heritage character.

AJAYPAL 26

Raja Ajaypal, the founder of Ajmer in 1100, chose this rocky valley 16 kilometres away to spend his last years in worship and renunciation. He lived to be 100 years old. Killing animals or violence of any kind is forbidden in this valley, once deeply forested and rich in game.

Largely due to the efforts and the following of Brahmachari

Harbhajan Das, Ajaypal has received donations to restore it to its age-old beauty and importance. A temple to Ardhanarishvara is being constructed here. The road to Ajaypal leads out from below the hill of the Savitri Temple, meets a dusty road, and finally passes over a 'mountain of gold dust' which glitters in the sun.

Its boulders in conglomerate granite have a surreal and sculpturesque quality.

OTHER SITES OF INTEREST

There are some sites at Pushkar which have not been put on official *parikrama* lists simply because they are worshipped by the Gauda Brahmans, patronized and installed here by the royal house of Jaipur. But they are certainly worth a visit for their fine craftsmanship. The beautiful 108 Mahadev, Koteshvar Mahadev, Indra, Surya and Chandra temples, and the Bihari-ji Temple fall in this category.

Although the Bihari-ji Temple is on the list for the 7.5 *kos parikrama*, it remains unvisited and closed.

108 MAHADEV TEMPLE

The 108 Mahadev Temple dates back to 1203 according to a *shilalekha*, or stone inscription, outside its sanctum sanctorum. While the interior holds a large *yoni-patta* with a *chaturmukhi shivalinga*, the temple gets its name from the 108 *lingas* adorned by

Nandis which line the circumambulatory path on three sides like a beaded Shiva rosary.

KOTESHVAR MAHADEV TEMPLE

Though the Koteshvar Mahadev Temple is recent by comparison, its scale and workmanship are exemplary. Situated off the Gwalior Ghat, this large temple with a spacious courtyard was only 50 years old when Colonel Broughton visited it: "Of the modern temples [it] is by far the most remarkable both for the size and elegance of its structure and nature of its ornaments." It was funded by Anaji Scindia and the imposing temple was built by the Maratha general Gumanji Rao between 1809 and 1816. Its *panchmukhi shivalinga* is crowned with matted hair.

INDRA GHAT

The Indra Ghat seems contemporary with similar marble iconography from the traditional Khazane Walon ka Rasta in Jaipur where temple idols are carved. The large, white, multi-trunk elephant Airavata on whom Indra sits is particularly realistic and impressive.

This was once called Abhay Singh Ghat after a Rajput vassal of the Mughals. A temple to Kalyan-ji probably built by him was shifted to Gau Ghat while another to Indra still exists and gives the ghat its name. The steps have been restored by Rajasthan Tourism. The temple at Indra Ghat also houses marble idols of Shiva-Parvati and a large Nandi carved in Jaipur. Smaller images of Ganesha and Kartikeya flank the main figures. Instead of the usual *abhishekhapatra* which

hangs above the *shivalinga* for ablutions, a clumsy pipe has now been added for this function.

CHANDRA & SURYA GHAT

A unique temple to Chandra and Surya, the moon and sun gods, was raised by Divan Shyam Lal Kayastha of Jaipur in 1908. One of the finest pieces of design and craftsmanship is the silver sun-and-moon image damascened in gold. The crescent moon affixed on a wall like a deity, shows a small, personified sun with its golden rays radiating in all directions held by a larger crescent moon. The Chandra and Surya Ghats were built by two brothers –

with the maharajas of Jaipur – Bakshi Sundar Lal Kayastha and Divan Shyam Lal Kayastha.

GANAPATI TEMPLE

Among the shops which line the Sadar Bazar along the *parikrama*

marg is a striking one-room temple of a giant Ganesha flanked by his wives Riddhi and Siddhi who wave fly whisks at him. All pasted in silver leaf foil, it makes an arresting and clean graphic image among the street clutter.

PATHVARI MATA

"Common people do not pray, they ask," Abraham Lincoln had once so aptly observed. If one were to go further and search – what is it that they ask for? – many of the temples and the gods or goddesses would have their justifications for the fields of magnanimity they represent. Pathvari Mata, or the goddess of stones, answers every pilgrim who burdened by the anxieties of joint families, yearns for a separate home. Between Bhavan Bhairon and Mahaprabhu-ji ki Baithak stands a *barh* tree. Below it, placing stones, one over the other, is a symbolic form of worship to the goddess of stone, who ensures that soon the worshipper will build a house of his/her own. The tree above symbolizes shelter.

MAN GHAT

Man Ghat is named after Raja Man Singh I of Jaipur, general of Akbar's armies and one of his nine jewels. "To him," writes Colonel James Tod, "Akbar was indebted for half his triumphs." In 1911, the historian Har Bilas Sarda noted that its ghats were "completely destroyed.... Attached to it is the Man Mandir, a square, cloistered building of brick and mortar, ruined and tenantless, save for the bats which alone inhabit it...it is hoped [it will] receive the attentive regard of the Jaipur State, the brightest page of whose history is the record of the exploits of Raja Man." This wish was only half-answered. After the formation of Rajasthan, this became the state government's property and is now a simple hotel of the Rajasthan Tourism Development Authority.

AKHAND PITHESHVAR ASHRAM

Half-way up the eastern hills which girdle Pushkar, lies the Akhand Pitheshvar Ashram where Swami Lehranand Chitrakoot presides. The Pandavas of the Mahabharata are believed to have visited this scenic spot from where a sadhu points towards the Sarovar lake.

SHAHI MASJID

Once a temple to Keshorai-ji stood here on an imposing height. This was destroyed to make way for a mosque, raised by Aurangzeb in the name of his father Shah Jahan or it may simply have been named Shahi Masjid – suggesting an imperial mosque. Fearing that the idol would be destroyed, the deity was removed overnight and carried far into the adjoining kingdom of Bundi. Desecrated idols and broken pillars lie strewn about. An impressive temple was raised there at Keshorai Patan, in the beginning of the 18th century. In vengeance for this vandalism, the priests of Pushkar seem to have now blocked the mosque's access to the lake. When the Keshorai Temple was razed to the ground and the Shahi Masjid raised in its place, one of the Parashara Brahmans supposedly agreed to convert to Islam and be the *khadim*, or caretaker. He was renamed Bundu Shah, and it is said that till date, it is his descendants who have taken care of the daily prayers at the mosque. The current *khadim* seems totally unaware of any such history.

PHOTOGRAPHER'S NOTE

The hot-air balloon from which the photographer took the aerial pictures.

As a young boy, my love for nature and outdoor life was never ending. Creating models, singing and painting came naturally to me. I believe that talents are inherited, these cannot be acquired, however, one can learn and polish these acquired skills. Painting was one of my first loves. Besides the issue of what and how to paint, what interested me was the frame itself: what I could capture within a contained space. This interest seems most naturally to have graduated to photography.

I admired the work of Henri Cartier Bresson, who shot 'off the cuff', so to say, but was a master of composition. His frames are legendary and he certainly carried his camera to amazing places and situations.

My own initiation came in 1990 when I bought my first SLR camera and happened to see the first photography exhibition of S Paul who I met thereafter. Subsequently, as a guru and companion, we travelled on long journeys and I learnt a great deal from him along with shooting a lot of black-and-white photographs.

In the mid-1990s, I decided to visit the magical site of Pushkar. It is among the most photographed events, and yet one is drawn to it, first from the initial curiosity of a beginner and later by its full-scale magnetism.

After several visits to Pushkar, I met Aman Nath in New Delhi, in order to show my work to him and evince his interest in my photographs. Being a Rajasthan-buff, he displayed great enthusiasm and appreciation – especially for my aerial balloon shots. What he didn't know was my narrow escape when the hot-air balloon collapsed. There was a great commotion: a hundred-thousand people running in all directions. Rather than click that picture I have carried it in my mind as I immediately got involved in looking after the injured!

Eventually I began to see Pushkar from a different, wider perspective which brought more objectivity to my work. Together, we made several visits to Pushkar, meeting and spending time with the rural folk, the nobility as well as the neighbouring royalty. Seeing the historical, mythological and ethnographical aspects of Pushkar was an altogether wonderful experience.

Now the result is in your hands, for your eyes to see and read.

— RAJAN KAPOOR, September 2005
rajankapoor@goldenpeacock.com

AUTHOR'S NOTE & ACKNOWLEDGEMENTS

I first visited Pushkar in 1974, a year after finishing college, invited by my friend Romi Chopra. That was the time of the flower generation when bell-bottoms and beads mattered much and Pushkar had the fresh colour of hippies. Having just completed my Masters in history from St Stephen's College, Delhi, I thought I had had my fill of the subject. I remember seeing things superficially: temples for temples, camels for camels and the beauty of the Rajasthanis as pure seduction. At the first level, all the pictures I carried back in my mind were giant postcards, and all tales from mythology or history were just tales. My following visits with Francis Wacziarg – during and after other books on Rajasthan – brought me closer to the sands of Pushkar, epitomizing the sands of time. I became interested in the hills and caves that lay beyond the nucleus of the scintillating lake. I was aware that there was more, but not certain if I would ever have the inclination and the opportunity to explore the Pushkar riddle.

The opportunity was to come when Rajan Kapoor contacted me with his photographs of Pushkar. Even at first glance, some were rather fresh views of a much-clicked subject. His aerial views, from a hot-air balloon, were particularly alluring. They elevated the human viewpoint to the creator's point of view – or at least as we imagine it from the terrestrial world. A spiritual subject like a pilgrimage needed an original approach. One cannot discover or research till the urge is compelling and self-motivated. I first reviewed the large stock of photographs which Rajan had amassed over seven years, then set out to look beyond the layman's eyes and unlayer things which most people do not bother to explore. I met the wise old men of the area, read obscure books and took the less-travelled routes to make some stunning discoveries. I did push Rajan to climb tedious peaks and when he showed a reluctance, I took his camera and trekked up myself. Each of us had our own eye for the smaller picture, which we saw within the larger whole. It was important to bring out the vision and scale of history in shaping a Hindu pilgrimage, possibly over several millennia.

These millennia have also been witness to the undeniable truth of belief in God or gods. This belief is older than history, and is reflected in the multi-religious society we live in now.

This book observes and records – but does not question – the fact that many who preach religion or thrive by the reputation of their pilgrimage, have made a business of it. Where history has been distorted, misrepresented or not probed, some issues have been raised. The text and pictures trace the beginnings of Pushkar and the history of those who have been associated with it through time. There are several grey areas between mythology, history and oral transformations over generations, and the human tendency to add, exaggerate and embroider over whatever we know. These facets have been explored as a storyteller's carry-over from one century to the other. But the patterns which create and market the myths in themselves make an interesting study – no matter whether they are of Hindu, Muslim, Jain, or Christian origin.

Let this book take you to the eternal joy of being at the Rajasthani fair of Pushkar.

IN PUSHKAR I am first most grateful to Yogendra Singh Rathore of Nand for taking complete charge of us at the asking of his brother DSP Gyanendra of Behror. He gave of his time while also generously lending his family jeep and driver Ganesh Ram, to reach many places which are otherwise quite inaccessible. Later, Jayendra Rathore's help in filling the photography gaps, was much appreciated. My knowledge about Pushkar would have been incomplete without having met Kalyan Mal Shastri-ji, a walking encyclopaedia of the pilgrimage. Unfortunately, he passed away before seeing the book in print. To his protégé, Radhey Shyam Kala, our constant guide on every trip, goes my gratitude for introducing me to all the Parasharas and Gauda Brahmans so that each could tell his own tale. Janardhan Sharma was particularly kind in sharing his wisdom with much modesty. Pandit Lal Maharaj-ji's handbook on the *parikramas* was a good blueprint to begin the research. Anantprasad L Ganeriwal of the Old Rang-ji Temple took us under his fold to feed and pamper us on exhausted afternoons and to provide valuable information. Besides providing their input on the crocodiles, Govind Deo of Kharwa and his charming wife Kavita played host to us warmly and gracefully at the Pushkar Resort.

IN AJMER To Niranjan Arya, district magistrate and collector, and to Saurabh Srivastava, DSP, Rajan and I are particularly grateful for special permissions through the threatened high-security fair that post-September 11 had become in 2001. To the admirable Mugdha Sinha, I owe a personal tribute for her fortitude despite a recent tragedy, to make all permissions possible including photography from a raft and tyre float on the lake, hitherto not allowed to anyone. Dalel Singh of Bhinai asserted his right as an old friend to open all doors and introduce me to his fellow Istimrardars. To Pramod Chand Jain of the Nasiyan Temple for his cooperation and assistance to shoot the magical creation of his ancestors. For Onkar Singh Lakhawat's love of history and archiving, this book is richer and his passion to call a spade a spade today, deserves a cautioning attention for the future. To Jodha Ram Babar, curator of the Government Museum, Ajmer, I owe my gratitude for his willful cooperation. To Manjeet Singh (Monty) of Raipur and his father Karni Singh-ji for generous access to their rare books which they photocopied for me. To Dushyant Singh of Masuda for use of his old photographic postcards of Ajmer-Pushkar as well as of his family's agreement documents with the British Empire. To Sanjay Singh Badnor for his friendship and advice on the *dargah's* photography.

IN JAIPUR To Rajeeva Swarup for his generosity in letting us use the Rajasthan Tourism facilities at Pushkar and Arvind Mayaram for permission to shoot at the Government Museum, Ajmer. To the ever-helpful Lalit Pawar, I owe gratitude for the sharing of his knowledge on Rajasthan; to Tripti Pandey for identifying the dancers and their dance forms and to Hari Narain Ghiya for his warmth and willingness in finding supporting visual material from Rajasthan.

IN JODHPUR To Shraddha Chauhan for advice on the spiritual aspects of Brahma, Pushkar and the cow.

IN KISHANGARH To Brajraj Singh for the warm and open access to his home and his knowledge of history as the chief Rathore of Ajmer-Merwara.

IN DELHI To Om Arora for suggesting to Rajan that he and I collaborate on this book. I owe more than just a thank you to Harveen Kapoor, meeting whom was one of the rewards of this book. She introduced me to the work of Shashi Shekhar Sharma who later became a friend and guide in understanding the depths of Hinduism without being defensive about its assimilative reach. To Namita Gokhale's good advisory sense which combined a friend's bias with a critic's ruthlessness, this book owes some of its secular, Hindu forthrightness. To the erudite Dr PS Dwivedi, my college professor of ancient Indian history, I owe my beginnings of that learning curiosity for digging into history. To reconnect with his wisdom after three decades was a true pleasure. When I thanked him deeply and profusely for all his help, corrections and contribution, he moved me with his humility, "I learnt so much from reading your book." It is also the time to thank the late Roop Narain Shastri whose help in procuring old illustrations, manuscripts, books and paintings has helped enrich the text and visual material in this book. To Mahendra Pratap Singh for re-shaping the many manifestations of this book with patience and calm till it was re-laid again in Mumbai by Jatin Lad, Jagdish Limbachiya and finally Nidhi Sah who attended to its minutest design details under Meera Ahuja's direction. Vani Bahl's support on the net and on the trip to Pushkar as well as her continued positive energy certainly merits a mention.
To Tomy Abraham, who coordinated all the visual material over three years, this book is indebted for much of its cohesion. To Lavanya Ray whose suggestions during a preliminary editing were very helpful. To GC Jain, Rajiv and Sanjiv Jain of RS Books, a treasure house of rare archival material, my thanks for providing free access to their wide collection; to Sqn Ldr C Darshan for guiding me.

IN BHOWALI To Salim and Jitendra Malkani for timely help in putting my manuscripts on CD so that they could travel light to Delhi.

IN NEEMRANA To Ramesh Dhabhai and his team for holding fort as well as his father Bajrang Lal-ji Dhabhai in Mandawa for help with the neglected history of the Gurjaras.

IN RAMGARH, KUMAON A large part of this book was written here, my gratitude to KS Mehra, to Suresh Darmwal and Rajdeep Arya and all the Neemrana Hotel staff for their warmth and care.

IN MUMBAI At India Book House to Padmini Mirchandani for making me feel so much at home and to Meera Ahuja for steering the book from its formative stages – often chaotic – to much order. Without her eye for and attention to editing and design details, the book would not be what it has become. The scholarship of Biswajeet Rath who edited the first manuscript and to Shernaz Vasunia, who pointed out and discussed many aspects in the fine-tuning of the text, posterity will, I hope be grateful that history was not just recorded, but with much attention to minute details. To Nikita Mehta who coordinated the discordant material into some coherence.

To Sanjay Bhattacharyya, who accompanied me so willingly to Pushkar and then produced an admirably detailed watercolour, I am indebted as will be all initiated readers, since his work literally transports them to an aerial visit of the complex pilgrimage.

To Francis Wacziarg for the liberal use of his office, for access to his rare French books on India and his continuous support over several years in making this project possible at all levels and – simply for being.

To my mother, who encouraged in me the boundless spirit of enquiry and adventure, I am grateful for taking good care of Aadya on my long absences.

— AMAN NATH, September 2005
aman_nath2002@yahoo.co.in

Aman Nath at Pushkar 30 years ago!

GLOSSARY

abhishekha the process of anointing. Traditionally, *abhishekha* would involve ritual washing of votive objects with various auspicious fluids such as milk, ghee and pure water.
abhishekhapatra pot with a minute perforation at the bottom from which drops of water constantly fall on the image.
achhut literally, 'untouchable', referring to a lower caste.
advaita literally, 'not two', *advaita* derives from Vedanta philosophy, and is often described as a monistic or non-dualistic approach. Adi Shankaracharya was the first to consolidate the principles of *advaita.*
aghanya that which cannot be slaughtered.
ahankara ego.
aj goat.
akhand bhashma sacred ashes.
amria possibly originating from *amar* (immortal), this term is used for the goats in Pushkar.
anusvara syllable which renders a chant permanent and indestructible.
apsara nymph.
arka literally, a 'ray of light', usually stands for the sun.
arsha-tirtha place of pilgrimage which is associated with austerities, penances and sacrifices.
arti is a ritual in which light from a wick soaked in ghee is offered to one or more deities. Its origin may be traced to the Vedic concept of fire rituals.
ashvamedha yajna ancient Indian horse sacrifice performed by Hindu kings to celebrate their supremacy and for the posterity and fertility of their kingdoms.
asura-tirtha place of pilgrimage which is associated with the destruction of demons by the trinity (Brahma, Vishnu, Shiva).
atma can be translated as self, soul or ego. Beginning with Vedantic Hindu philosophy, the *atma* is regarded as an underlying metaphysical self. It is first seen in its current Hindu usage in the Upanishads, some of which date back to 1000 BCE. The word *atma* is interpreted by some schools as the 'main essence' of man, as his 'highest self'.
aughar unfinished act.
baati wheat-flour preparation shaped like a ball.
Baisakhi Purnima full moon in the month of *Baisakh*. *Baisakhi* marks the beginning of the new Spring year and the end of the harvest in India. *Baisakhi Purnima* falls on the first day of *Baisakh* and is the beginning of the Lunar calendar. It usually falls on April 13, falling on April 14 once every 36 years.
baori stepwell.
baradari room with 12 doors, designed to allow free draught of air through it.
barat groom's entourage.
behrupia one who uses different disguises to entertain and earn a living.
belcha accoutrement for a camel, in the form of a decorated rope.
bhakta disciple.
bhakti devotion.
bhashma see *akhand bhashma.*
bhikshu fully-ordained Buddhist monk.
bodhisattva in Buddhism, one who is motivated by compassion and seeks enlightenment.
brahm equivalent to Brahmanda, or cosmos (originating from the cosmic egg).
brahmakshetra literally, 'land of Brahma', this term is used in the Mahabharata and the Puranas.
Brahmanda vast cosmic space. See also *brahm.*
brahmashirastra celestial weapon.
chakravartin universal ruler.
chapa bow.
chaturmukha four-faced, refers to Brahma with four heads.
chaupad ancient board game.
chaurasi metal adornment for a camel.
chheuti four-point saddle for a camel.
chillum smoking pipe.
churma grainy powder.
daiva-tirtha place of pilgrimage created by the gods, mainly the male deities of the trinity.
darbar royal court, council for administering affairs of the state or ceremonial gathering.
dargah tomb of a Muslim saint.
deg cauldron.
devayana path leading to the gods.
dharamshala literally, 'rest house', often developed into a centre of religious learning.
dhuni sacred fire.
ekam advaityam symbolizing one essence and no other.
gangri rake.
garbha-griha literally 'womb home or chamber', refers to the sanctum sanctorum, where the image of the god is housed.
godhuli dusk.
gopuram rising tower at the entrance of a temple, usually decorated with carvings.
gufa cave.
gul flower.
gulab rose.
gulkand paste of rose petals eaten as a mild laxative in a *paan*, or betel leaf.
gurudwara holy place of worship for Sikhs.
hansa swan, vehicle of Brahma.
haveli mansion, usually used in the Rajasthani context.
hiranyagarbha signifies intelligence, the supreme lord of the universe, the Hindu primordial being. He was the primeval seed from which Brahma was born.
hukamnamah royal order.
jagir small territory received as recognition of services rendered.
jagirdari system of private landlords prevalent in the British period. This system was abolished in 1960.
janapada province or state.
janitra birthplace, place of origin, home, origin. Also refers to generative or procreative matter.
jharokha projecting balcony with a domed or vaulted roof.
jhul ornament worn by the camel.
jugad public transport system.
juti footwear.
jyotirlinga shrine where Shiva is worshipped in the form of a *jyotirlinga* or 'linga of light'. There are traditionally 12 *jyotirlinga* shrines in India.
kabaddi team sport primarily played in South Asia. The name is derived from the Hindi word meaning 'holding breath'.
kalapasa literally, 'noose of time', held by Yama the lord of death.
kalpa four *kalpas* are the four periods of time that a world is said to repeatedly undergo. A *kalpa* consists of a period of 1,728,000 solar years called *adi sandhi*, followed by 14 *manvantaras* and *sandhi kalas*. Two *kalpas* constitute a day and night of Brahma. The life cycle of Brahma is 100 years of Brahma, or 311 trillion years.
kamandala literally, 'water pot', refers to Brahma's *kamandala* which denotes his meditative and spiritual qualities.
kanphata literally, 'a slice in the ear', applies to the Gorakhnathis in Pushkar who split the cartilages of their ears with a knife.
kapala skull or forehead.
Kartik Purnima full moon (*purnima*) of the month of *Kartik* (October-November).
katha story or reading.
kathi wooden saddle for a camel.
kevalagyan unique knowledge attained by Mahavira, the Jain *tirthankara.*
kheeng traditional tattoo used to distinguish camels at the Pushkar fair.
khel sport.
khichra paste of rose-millet.
kirti-sthambha tower (column) of victory.
kshetra region.
kund tank.
linga the phallic representation of Shiva, the *linga* symbolizes both the creative and destructive power of the lord.
lokapalas guardians of the four directions. They are usually placed in pairs at the entrance to temples. The four *lokapalas* in Hinduism are Indra (east), Yama (south), Varuna (west) and Kubera (north).
madrasa institution that offers courses, individual study and programs on Islam using the methodology of traditional scholars.

mahasabha general assembly.
mahatma great individual, also refers to the supreme spirit.
mahayuga equivalent to one cycle of the Satya, Treta, Dvapara and Kali *yugas*, which form a total of 4.32 million solar years. This is one year in the life of Brahma.
malpua traditional syrupy dessert.
manasthambha mighty pillar, with some religious significance attached to it.
manusha-tirtha place of pilgrimage which is created by man.
matha religious establishment.
maya illusion.
mela fair.
melkhuri layer of wool or thick cotton placed on a camel's back.
mlechha refers to a foreigner, and mentioned in the Vana Parva of the Mahabharata.
mohra neckband for a camel.
mundra decorative motifs cut out of camel's hair.
nadi channel.
nastika atheist.
nevri ornament worn on the front of the ankles of the camel's front legs.
odhni long piece of cloth that is used by women to cover the head and upper body.
paan betel leaf.
padmak yog place of celestial importance. The term is used in the Puranas to refer to the Pushkar lake.
padmasana literally, 'lotus pose', refers to yogic seating posture.
pagra stirrup.
pala see *lokapala.*
pancha kalyanaka five luminous events in the life of Mahavira.
panchayat village committee which delivers judgement on various disputes.
panchmukhi five-faced, referring to the five-headed Brahma.
parandi hair ornament.
parbatsari goat breed.
paridhi enclosure.
parikrama circumambulation, often signifying a specific route.
path religious reading or sermon.
peeth a centre of religious or mythological importance.
piao roadside facility for drinking water.
pinda-daan offering to the ancestors.
pitamaha elderly figure, referring to Brahma.
pitamahasara waters of the *pitamaha*, i.e., Brahma.
pitrayana path leading to the 'fathers' (as against *devayana*, a path leading to the gods).
pitri ancestor.
prajayanitra progenitor.
prakriti nature.
prasad offering.
prayashchita daan offering as a repentance of past deed(s).
punya virtue, merit or good deed.
purusha primeval being, single male energy.
purusharthas 'goals of life'. The *purusharthas* are *kama*, *artha*, dharma and moksha.
pushpa flower.
rajas originally meaning atmosphere, air or firmament. *Rajas* is considered to be an attribute of Brahma and has been translated to mean overactivity or turmoil.
rajoguna literally, 'methods of a king', leads to activity and bondage.
rani queen.
ravaana departure.
rehgar low caste of leather workers.
sadhvi female householder who has voluntarily renounced the world.
samadhi burial place.
sangam meeting point, confluence.
sanyasi one who has renounced the materialistic world.
sarga chapter or section in a text.
sarovar lake, water body.
sattvaguna good trait.
shaikh refers to a revered personage and applies to Muslim saints belonging to various Sufi orders.
Sharad Purnima festival that is observed on the night of the full moon in the month of *Ashvina* (September-October). The moon-god is also the lord of herbs, seeds, the Brahmans, waters and *nakshatras*, or constellations. It is believed that on *Sharad Purnima*, *amrit*, or elixir, is showered on the earth by the moon through his beams.
shatkumarika celestial goddess.
shikhar literally, tower or peak, represents a style of temple architecture.
shilalekha stone inscription.
shivalinga see *linga.*
shloka verse that is recited in Sanskrit literature.
shradh ritualistic ceremony observed annually to commemorate the death of a family member.
shrauta class of later Vedic literature.
siddha spiritual perfection or enlightenment.
silsila chain of transmission (within a religious order).
singhara one of the decorative elements in the camel's saddle.
soma intoxicating drink, originating in Vedic literature.
soni jeweller.
soria adornment placed around the camel's mouth.
sudarshan chakra wheel-shaped weapon of Krishna (or Vishnu).
sunnud agreement.
svargavasa residing in heaven.
tamas darkness or inertia, sometimes interpreted as the state of ignorance.
tamoguna 'mode of ignorance, or darkness', characterized by dissolution and destruction, madness, indolence and sleep.
tamra-patra copper plate.
tang sheep wool strap.
tantrika practitioner of tantra.
tapa Hindu meditation technique. See also *tapas*.
tapas literally, 'heat', *tapas* refers to the concentrated spiritual exercises to attain God. The practice of *tapas* implies self-discipline, penance and austerity.
telia goat breed.
thali round utensil similar to a plate.
tharas leather cushions acting as the topmost layer in the camel's saddle.
tibari arched door gallery.
tilak mark worn on the forehead as a symbol of reverence towards the almighty. Usually made of sandal paste, the *tilak* is applied in various shapes by different religious communities.
tirtha place of pilgrimage, usually with a bathing place.
tirtha purohit religious community or priest situated at a pilgrimage site, which caters to the ritualistic requirements of the pilgrims.
tirthaguru leading pilgrimage site.
tirthankara refers to the enlightned one in Jainism. There are 24 *tirthankaras* with Mahavira being the last.
trimurti Hindu trinity, referring to Brahma (the creator), Vishnu (the preserver), and Shiva-Maheshvara (the destroyer). These three gods are often depicted as a single deity in Hindu philosophy.
triveni confluence.
urdhvalinga tapasya literally, 'phallus erectum', a manifestation of Shiva worship. This form can be traced back to the Harappan civilization (2500–1700 BCE).
vahana vehicle.
vanaspati shakti vegetal power.
vapi tank.
vatika forest.
vibhuti holy ash.
yajamaan one who performs the sacrifice.
yajna literally, 'worship, prayer, or offering', a *yajna* is performed to appease the gods. The performance is signified by offering oblations to a sacrificial fire, or *agni*.
yoni literally translated from Sanskrit as the 'female reproductive organ', *yoni* is considered symbolic of the goddess Shakti, and in a religious and philosophical context, it refers to creativity.
yuga refers to an age or epoch. In Hindu thought, the cycle of life is composed of four *yugas*: Satya, Treta, Dvapara and Kali. Each *yuga* has a particular attribute: Satya signifies *dhyana* (meditation), Treta denotes *yajna* (sacrifice), Dvapara refers to *archana* (worship), Kali is the age of *daana* or donations. See also *mahayuga*.

SELECT BIBLIOGRAPHY

Agrawala, Vasudeva S. *Shiva Mahendra: The Great God.* Varanasi: Veda Academy, 1966.

Ali, Salim. *The Book of Indian Birds.* Mumbai: Bombay Natural History Society & Oxford University Press, Delhi, 2002 (Thirteenth Edition).

Bailey, Greg. *The Mythology of Brahma.* Delhi: Oxford University Press, 1983.

Banerjee, JN. *The Classical Age,* HCIP, vol III. Bhartiya Vidya Bhavan, 1970.

Basham, AL. *The Wonder that was India: A Survey of the Culture of the Indian Sub-continent before the Coming of Muslims.* Calcutta: Rupa & Co, 1967 (Reprint).

Bhardwaj, SM. *Hindu Places of Pilgrimage in India: A Study in Cultural Geography.* Delhi: Thompson Press (India) Limited & University of California Press, Berkeley, Los Angeles, London, 1973.

Bhattacharya, NN. *The Geographical Dictionary: Ancient and Early Medieval India.* New Delhi: Munshiram Manoharlal Publishers, 1991.

Chauhan, Rana Alihassan. *Gurjaron Ka Sankshipt Itihaas.* Translated by Omprakash Gurjar & Chaudhary Shaukat Jung Gurjar. Yamunanagar, Haryana: Gurjar Ekta Parishad.

Currie, PM *The Shrine and Cult of Muin al-din Chisti of Ajmer.* Delhi: Oxford University Press, 1989.

De Jancigny, Dubois & Xavier Raymond. *Inde.* Paris: Firmin Didot Frères, Èditeurs, M DCCC XLV.

Dey, Nandoo Lal. *The Geographical Dictionary of Ancient and Medieval India.* New Delhi: Cosmos Publications, 1979.

Dixon, CJ (Lt Col). *Sketch of Mairwara.* London: Smith, Elder, and Co, 1850.

Dowson, John. *A Classical Dictionary of Hindu Mythology.* New Delhi: Oriental Books Reprint Corporation, 1973.

Eck, Diana L. *Banaras: City of Light.* London: Routledge & Kegan Paul, Melbourne & Henley, 1983.

Francis, Charles Richard. *Sketches of Native Life in India with Views in Rajpootana, Simlah, Etc, Etc.* London: Meldola, Cahn & Co, 1848.

Garrett, John. *A Classical Dictionary of India.* 1871. New Delhi: Munshiram Manoharlal Publishers,1986 (Oriental Reprint).

Gibson, Jack. *As I Saw It: Records of a Crowded Life in India, 1937-1969.* New Delhi: Mukul Prakashan, 1976.

Goendka, Jaydalal. *Padmapurana.* Gorakhpur: Gita Press.

Goradia, Prafull. *The Saffron Book.* New Delhi: Contemporary Targets Ltd, 2002.

Gupta N, P Spear & RE Frykenberb. *The Delhi Omnibus.* New Delhi: Oxford University Press, 2002.

Hart-Suiker, Dolf. *Sadhus: Holy Men of India.* London: Thames & Hudson,1993.

Kane, PV. *History of the Dharmashastras: Ancient and Medieval, Religious and Civil Law,* 5 vols. Poona: Bhandarkar Oriental Research Institute.

Khanna, Amar Nath. *Pilgrim Shrines of India: Mythology, Archaeology, History and Art.* New Delhi: Aryan Books International, 2003.

Kipling, Rudyard. *Kim.* 1901. London: Penguin Popular Classics, 1994 (Reprint).

Lakhawat, Onkar Singh. *Barhath Naraharidas.* New Delhi: Kendriya Sahitya Akademi, 2003.

Le Bon, Gustave. *Les Civilisations De L'Inde.* Paris: Librairie De Firmin-Didot Et cie, 1887.

Mani, Vettam. *Puranic Encyclopaedia.* Delhi: Motilal Banarsidass Publishers, 1993.

Mansingh, Surjit. *Historical Dictionary of India.* New Delhi, Bombay, Hyderabad: Vision Books, 1998.

Oppert, G. *On the Weapons, Army Organisation, and Political Maxims of the Ancient Hindus: With Special Reference to Gunpowder & Firearms.* New Delhi: Cosmo, 2005.

Pathak, VS. *Smarta Religious Tradition.* Meerut: Kusumanjali Prakashan. 1987.

Pushkar Catalogue. Government of Rajasthan.

Report on the Census of 1891, vol 2 ("The Castes of Marwar"). Jodhpur: by the Order of the Marwar Darbar, 1894.

Rousselet, Louis. *India and its Native Princes: Travels in Central India and in the Presidencies of Bombay and Bengal.* London: Bickers & Son, 1878.

Sarda, Har Bilas. *Ajmer: Historical and Descriptive.* Ajmer: Fine Art Printing Press, 1941.

Sharma, Shashi S. *Oh My God: The Nature of Divine Faultlines.* New Delhi: Rupa & Co, 2002.

Shekhavat, Thakur Surjan Singh Jhajhar. *Kharwa ka Itihaas.* Ajmer: The Diamond Jubilee Press, 1998.

Sinha, Surajit & Saraswati Baidyanath. *Ascetics of Kashi: An Anthropological Exploration.* Varanasi: NK Bose Memorial Foundation, 1978.

Stutley, Margaret. *The Illustrated Dictionary of Hindu Iconography.* London: Routledge & Kegan Paul, Boston, Melbourne & Henley. 1985.

Stutley, Margaret & James. *A Dictionary of Hinduism: Its Mythology, Folklore and Development 1500 BC-1500 AD.* London: Routledge & Kean Paul, Melbourne & Henley, 1977.

Thackston, Wheeler M, ed. *Jahangirnama, Memoirs of Jahangir, Emperor of India.* New York: Oxford University Press in association with the Freer Gallery of Art & Arthur M Sackler Gallery, 1999.

Tod, James (Lt Col). *Travels in Western India, Embracing a Visit to the Sacred Mounts of the Jains and the Most Celebrated Shrines of the Hindu Faiths.* London: WH Allen & Co, 1839.

Tod, James (Lt Col). *Annals and Antiquities of Rajasthan,* 3 vols. Oxford: Oxford University Press, 1920.

Varma, Ratanlal. *Bhartiya Sanskriti ke Rakshak.* Shikarpur, Uttar Pradesh: Bhartiya Gurjar Parishad.

Waddington, CW. *Indian India.* London: Jarrolds Publishers, MCMXXXIII.

Walker, Benjamin. *Hindu World: An Encyclopaedic Survey of Hinduism,* 2 vols. New Delhi: Munshiram Manoharlal Publishers, 1983.

Welch, Stuart Cary. *Room for Wonder: Indian Painting during the British Period 1760-1880.* New York: American Federation of Arts, Rizzoli International Publications Inc, 1978.

Besides the dictionaries and encyclopaedias of Hindu mythology which talk of other Brahma temples, Greg Bailey, an Australian scholar, has done extensive research during the 1970s and 1980s on the neglected Creator. In his book, The Mythology of Brahma, *he has, among other things, attempted to arrive at an understanding of Brahma's role in the relationship between the creation and organization of the universe – creation by progeniture and creation by closing the cycle of death, granting boons to demons, wayward sexuality and finally preserving dharma in the three worlds.*

STOP PRESS!

During the *yajna*, once Brahma's angered wife Savitri had settled on Ratnagiri hill in Pushkar, her mortal devotees may have thought that all marital issues were resolved. But as recently as in 1984, Mahant Laharpuri of the Brahma Temple filed a suit against Benugopal Sharma, head priest of the Savitri Temple. The former demanded the full earnings of his 'wife' during the five crowded days of the Pushkar fair. Just as this book was going to press, Sanjay Singh Badnor reported from Ajmer in *The Times of India* that OP Bansal, the counsel for the defendant Benugopal, fought Laharpuri's claim with the argument that since Brahma had deserted his wife, he could not insist on any rights from her. Moreover, since Savitri was Brahma's deserted wife she should be given alimony instead by the Brahma Temple. This plea was rejected by the court because the case involves idols who, it seems, are perpetual minors under the Hindu law!

CREDITS

t: top, b: bottom, c: center, l: left, r: right, 1: 1st column, 2: 2nd column, 3: 3rd column, 4: 4th column

COLLECTIONS

Aman Nath 10t, 11 (t&b), 12b,13, 14 (t&b), 15, 16b, 22-23, 26, 28t, 37t, 39, 44b, 48, 57t, 59 (t&b), 98b, 166t, 189 (3t), 193 (1b), 199
Dalel Singh Bhinai 180,181
Dushyant Singh Masuda 178
Francis Wacziarg 10b, 12t, 44t, 51t
Govind Deo of Kharwa 179

ILLUSTRATIONS

Mahendra Singh 36 (*inset*), 183 (*inset*)

PHOTOGRAPHS

Aman Nath 19t, 21t, 24c, 27t, 28b, 29, 34-35, 36 (t&b), 37b, 49-50t, 54r, 55t, 58t, 59, 60, 61, 63 (Bhanvta Devi Temple, Nandrai Mata), 64 (Shiva Temple; Thanvla, Bhairav Nath, Bada Asan, Baval Mata, Makrol Mata/Markandeya Ashram, Lomash Rishi/Rojari Mata), 65 (Hanuman Baori, Bhat Baye, Bhuteshvar Mahadev, Neelkanth Mahadev, Vamdev Gufa), 73l, 93br, 94t, 98t, 99, 100, 101 (tr, bl&br), 110, 134t, 136 (tl&br), 138 (tl&tr), 139, 147tr, 152b, 159 (tr&br), 161, 163tr, 164-165, 183, 184 (t,1&3b), 188 (1t&c), 189 (1b, 2&4t), 191 (1b&2t), 192 (2b,3l&r), 193 (3t&b, 4t&c), 194 (1&2), 195 (1t, 4t&c), 196b
Government of Rajasthan 58b, 160b
Jayendra Rathore 64 (Badri Narayan Temple, Shri Ram Jharokha), 66 (Baba Ramdev), 190 (2t)
Mahendra Singh 51br, 64 (Adhar Shila), 134b, 191 (4t)
Neeraj Pant 16t
RS Books 56
Ram Singh Bir 108tr
Romi Chopra 197

PAINTING

Sanjay Bhattacharyya 63-66

INDEX

Page numbers in **bold** refer to text in boxes and captions

A Ganjifa card, depicting a herd of camels from the 18th or 19th century with the dull red background suggesting its Jaipur-Udaipur origins.

LOSING COUNT

When will they wisen up –
the gods, I mean?
Or won't they simply wisen us
from dream-sculpting more gods?

From flowing blood
beyond our veins?

Long we've shaped them
from little or large minds,
by large means, in simple tales,
in faces, concepts, revelations

Truly, we've lost track
of counting up to just One!

For God is God, and men are men
unknowingly unwise
breeding fertile as their land
their overbearing skies
with myriad names
from countless times

Gods of many moulds pagan
heathen, still being revealed!
Go back to those who cast you,
and let us mortals freely breathe.

— AMAN NATH